A GOOD VIEW OF GOD

B R E N T   R.   T A Y L O R

page art by Lauren Taylor - graphic designer

A Good View of God

Brent Taylor

Copyright 2015

Cover art work by Lauren Taylor

Editor: Greg Taylor

CONTENTS

Preface

I began collecting stories the summer of my eleventh birthday. It began with a rambling conversation written in my memory like electric script on an etch-a-sketch that nobody bothered to shake clean.

It was a soft summer evening and the rolling asphalt hills of our neighborhood contained the entire universe. We were unaware theologians looking for trouble walking the streets and talking about the origination of the universe. Schoolboys wearing Levis and P.F. Flyers, while Mungo Jerry sang, "In the Summertime," on a street that looked like every white bread neighborhood between Santa Monica and Albany in 1970.

The world hadn't shrunk yet, it was still unfathomably huge, our neighborhood small, although everything we wanted was a short walk outside our door, bikes, woods and water, and girls. In the midst of that lush evening, when the entire world was at our beck and call, when we didn't know what hurt yet, we looked into the heavens. There were rockets in space, jets in the blue, and Chinese fire drills in the streets, and we had a gleam in our eyes with nothing yet to regret. In the midst of a conversational lull, someone shattered the glass wall separating my church friends and my school friends with a question, "Do you believe in God?"

These were my school buddies and we didn't go to church together. It was the first authentic conversation I had about transcendence, about a Creator, about what happens when we die. A meandering conversation unfiltered by adult oversight, transparent and wide-eyed, started with someone noticing the stars sparkling on the horizon, through the soft evening shadows, beautiful, worth noticing. "Hey, look at the stars! The sun isn't down yet and we can see them." We walked along for a while without speaking, looking at this beauty which we couldn't name, waiting for more signs.

We didn't solve the metaphysical questions of the universe that evening, but it began a conversation that I've since carried with me everywhere I go. It's not an Einsteinian quest for a theory of everything, but rather a question about the intersection of space/time with the dirt we kick up walking around on earth. Do the planes of the Heavens intersect with the plains of Oklahoma, Calcutta, and Jerusalem?

I've been walking along trying to name the beauty of that evening ever since. This book is just another attempt to name those moments , brilliant points of illumination, the caressing beauty of heaven touching earth, and to feel the mysterious wonder of places with more dimensions than I can understand. And sometimes, if I'm really calm, I see it as clearly as twinkling stars, competing against the sun of a midsummer's evening.

1

Kiss me like that

How on earth are you ever going to explain in terms of chemistry and physics so important a biological phenomenon as first love? ~ *Albert Einstein*

I grew up with Kevin Arnold of the Wonder Years except I rooted for the Packers instead of the Jets. And in the midst of the Sixties, while the tie-dye enlightened were *turning on, tuning in and dropping out*, I was simply roaming about my neighborhood trying to figure out the meaning of life. Our home was a split level that my Dad, a home builder, constructed in 1963. It had a small hole in the foyer linoleum the shape of Africa which I dug with a safety pin because I was bored, an elm tree with a split trunk creating an outdoor recliner we called the "Shady Rest", and tuna can golf cups buried throughout the backyard. We tested the limits of downhill biking on steep streets in the summer, we played touch football in autumn, and when serendipitous snow blew from the Oklahoma plains, we sledded down Suicide Hill stacked three high on a sled, crashing into ditches in a pile of rayon legs and woollen hands.

My friends and I roamed the woods using mischief to paint graffiti on a neighborhood canvas that could have been mistaken for time or a billboard or grinding boredom. We built fortresses in the woods behinds our homes, in the event of an invasion by the Soviet Union. We also pondered the deeper questions of supple formative minds, like whether or not Neil Armstrong had a good view of God while walking on the moon July 20, 1969. This was after all the dawning of the Age of Aquarius, and we wondered why we no longer felt revulsion around girls.

My first crush and heartbreak over a girl made as much sense as Dustin Hoffman and Anne Bancroft in *The Graduate*. She was twice my age, sophisticated, blond, shapely and fifteen. Like a dog chasing a car, I had no idea what a boyfriend did with a girlfriend, but I was a smitten seven-year old, jealous because the fifteen-year old twirler in the high school band loved my neighbor, Randy. He was the first pretty boy I knew, an olive-skinned Romeo, dark, handsome and sixteen to my short, pale and seven. I was as hopelessly in love as a seven-year old boy could possibly be.

Jan, who lived across the street in a red brick Cape Cod house with white trim, fell madly in love with Randy. I hated him for that, as did my neighborhood buddies. I had fond memories of Jan babysitting. We would sit on the couch while I leaned against her arm and she'd run her fingers through my hair as we watched Gilligan's Island. Or I would hang out at her house in the hip upstairs game room with the shag rug listening to "Oh, Sweet Pea," by Tommy Roe or The Temptations "My Girl" and wishing it were so.

Randy's sister, Christy, was the first girl I ever kissed. We found ourselves alone one day in the wood box in the backyard with the lid down. We were both five and hadn't a clue but had seen it done, so why not? And in the sixth grade, under a persimmon tree I kissed a girl, not passionately, but rather the thin-lipped front porch mannequin kiss. Kissing under the persimmon tree felt like eating a persimmon: not romantic at all, puckered, organic, indifferent.

I wasn't a participant in my first real kiss, only a spectator. I walked into the laundry room of Randy's house on the day they were leaving for good, the Ross family packed and ready to drive west to Colorado. My nemesis, my romantic rival, was finally leaving, and I thought the door to everlasting love was opening. But the door I opened to the Ross laundry room revealed a surreal scene, boy saying goodbye to girl. Jan's eyes were swollen and red, leaking emotion onto his shirt like rain skidding down a window pane, as she pulled away from a kiss and turned to look at me, an intruder to their farewell intimacy, their tangled goodbye. I discovered passion as a voyeur next to a washing machine, watching with envy, this weeping river of emotion dotted with red eyes and trembling lips, tightly hugged, wrapped in longing, hidden in shadows of whispered anguish.

That moment in the laundry room was my first lesson in kissing. Sure, I'd seen Julie Andrews kiss Christopher Plummer in the "could this be happening to me" kiss from the *Sound of Music* but this, this cloying evocative embrace framing the kiss was what made me want to kiss a girl. I wanted what those two had. A desperate longing to be held, loved, touched, cried over if I ever left town. It made me want to get a girl just so I could leave. Just once to have that feeling of someone wanting me desperately, tearing them to pieces. Yea, kiss me like that.

That's why we didn't like Randy, because he stole my girl. Besides, he stunk at sports, which established the neighborhood pecking order. We often played tackle football in the Gilchrist's front yard, their driveway one end zone and a sandstone retaining wall the other. This sometimes resulted in a touchdown and concussion, cutting short excessive celebration in our neighborhood. Randy had a front shirt pocket and none of the other guys did. In his shirt pocket he carried a pencil, none of the other guys did that either. One day while playing football Randy got tackled and slammed to the ground. When he got up, the pencil lead had stuck in his chest and he had a pencil protruding from the meaty upper part of his right breast. New girl moves into the neighborhood, gracefully twirling a baton in a leggy and frilly uniform, blond and beautiful…and the pretty boy with the pencil lead stuck in his chest gets the girl. At the age of seven I bore the guilt of envy and shame, a ten-commandment-sin in a mind too small to hold it.

Most of the guys in the neighborhood were older than me. I was in grade school and they were all junior high age. So they let me hang with them and when they called a football play in the huddle for me and pitched me the ball, they blocked extra hard so I could score. It made me feel like Jim Brown and I loved playing ball with them. It was the balm for my desire to belong to someone, or something, the healing that restored my seven-year old self-worth. But alas, they were not always the best role models.

They told me that dog food was like human food, just a little drier, and they dared me to take a bite. I did. It tasted like ground cardboard mixed with bran flakes with a hint of vermin hair. I spewed and ran furiously through the back door into the kitchen and drank a glass of cold water. Another time we were hanging out in the woods next to the creek. They had a tepid bottle of Coors and were passing it around the circle. When they asked if I wanted to try it, I said, "Sure, it's got to be better than dog food." I took the bottle and tipped it up, swilling the warm sudsy brew, swishing it around my mouth. I thought they had put dog pee in the bottle and it was another joke. They laughed at me, but insisted it was real beer and that I better not tell my parents about the beer.

My Mom was the neighborhood counselor, social director and peacemaker. She wanted to reform them all, take them to church, buy them an ice cream cone and tell them Jesus loved them, and that the world is beautiful and they could go to heaven. They rarely accepted the "come to church" invitation, but always accepted the invitation to Cheeseburger Night.

Mom would drag out the griddle and fry up a dozen cheeseburgers and the guys would infiltrate our home on a Friday night. I don't remember the conversation or games we played inside. We were always itching to get back outside into the neighborhood evening which masked our mischief. We played Kick-the-Can or we would get down in the ditches on either side of the road waiting for a car to approach on the black asphalt neighborhood streets. Then we'd rise up on either side of the ditch, pantomiming gangs pulling an unseen rope in a violent night tug-of-war...our silent struggle bringing the approaching car to a tentative stop, whereupon both sides would stand up dropping the invisible rope, laughing hilariously at the driver of the car foolish enough to be brought to a halt by an imaginary rope. Then we'd sprint down a side yard, jump a fence and make our way back home.

They were decent guys individually, but as a group became a rowdy and incorrigible wild bunch. The redemptive softer side was Cheeseburger Night. It was my Mom's simple plan to redeem the neighborhood gang. One night after we ate cheeseburgers, the guys meandered onto the front porch and I could hear murmuring between Gene and Charlie. I soon realized what was going down, they were going to pummel Randy. Randy began backing away toward his house, eyeing the guys, on the verge of either breaking into a run or crying. I don't remember what happened after that, just that Mom sensed the proceedings and came out on the front porch to send everyone home, allowing Randy to go home without getting pummelled. He didn't do anything wrong, other than get the girl we all wanted.

I remember those times as good ones, even though some things I learned about life were a little on the edge for a young boy. It took time to understand everything I learned growing up in that neighborhood. Warm beer and unrequited love both need spit out. The passion of a great kiss is like eternal bliss, sublime, a temple gate, the headwaters of a lovely river. Cheeseburgers taste better when eaten with friends. We become better people by simply inviting folks into our homes, sharing our lives as we mingle and are carried along in that stream of graceful love, even when we swim against the current.

God forgive me for all the things I just confessed and for all the things I left out. In an age before helicopter parents hovered in spiralling proximity, God gave me a cheeseburger party Mom who loved me with tenacious gentleness and gave me room to eat a little dog food and kiss a girl or two in the neighborhood of my youth. A neighborhood that provided me a good view of the sky and the moon and the stars, a good view of passion in a laundry room, and a good view of God seen not in burning bushes, but revealed by shared kisses and cheeseburgers, kick the can and flawed heroes who counted me as their friend.

2

The Boy, The Man, and Gravel Baseball

I could always hit. I learned to hit with a broomstick and a ball of tape and I could always get that bat on the ball.

~ *Stan Musial*

I've always loved baseball. Even though it's a team game, I found solitary ways to embrace its poetry. I was a baseball Walter Mitty, transported to Busch Stadium in St. Louis. I straddled the mound glaring at the batter with annoyed disdain. I emulated Bob Gibson, throwing a rubber baseball against the brick wall of our house, aiming at a strike zone drawn with a chunk of sandstone. Curled up next to the console radio doing homework in the evenings, I dreamed fantastic dreams, like Lucy entering Narnia through the wardrobe door. My fantasy was pitching in front of a big league crowd as Harry Caray called balls and strikes. I chased the gods of my youth, unshakable baseball heroes who were immovable blocks of granite, statues without flaws. But I soon learned that heroes turn to piles of stone, and from piles of stone, perfection rises once again.

During the autumn of 1968, the walls tumbled down in a heap. The Detroit Tigers squared off against my St. Louis Cardinals in the World Series. Since all the games were played during the day, I brought my transistor radio to school in hopes of listening on the playground during recess. My fourth grade teacher, Mrs. Karbosky, would never allow a broadcast of the World Series in her classroom, or so we thought. She brought an element of deportment to my Midwestern upbringing, an air of dignified carriage replete with reading glasses strung around her neck with a silver chain and an erect proud posture.

It was my first encounter with the upper class whom I'd never met personally but had read about in books like the Great Gatsby. I didn't know if Mrs. "K" was wealthy or was just socially aloof, but I was sure that the rich folk acted like she did. However, she had moments of humanity that defied her veneer of aloof formality. I skipped school once when Grandpa died, and I came back to her class the day after the funeral. Mrs. Karbosky expressed her condolences for the passing of my Grandfather, told me she was sorry. She seemed a little more human to me after that, like she knew I had a life outside her sterling fiefdom of a classroom.

Mrs. Karbosky made famous the expression, "Class, I would like your undivided attention." I had never heard anyone talk that way nor had I ever attempted to divide my attention purposely. So, I was shocked when she let me and a buddy listen to the 1968 World Series in the back of the classroom. Shocked because it broke her wooden rule of focused attention long before the advent of multi-tasking.

By sheer force of intellectual elegance, Mrs. Karbosky ruled over her 4th grade minions as the queen of proper behavior. I approached her desk with Stan to ask if we could listen to the World Series, frozen with the fear of her belittling my banal desire to listen to a silly game, to "*divide my attention*" as it were. To my amazement she said yes, so Stan and I huddled in the back of the classroom listening to Harry Caray and Jack Buck call the game as Bob Gibson dueled Mickey Lolich. During recess we took the transistor radio to the playground and listened in between taking turns at tetherball on the playground. The game still had a few innings left when the 3:00 bell dismissed us for the day, so I ran down the hall, burst out the double doors and sprinted two blocks to my home to watch the end of the game on television. The Cardinals lost that seventh and final game of the Series and I walked out my front door and yelled, "I hate the Tigers!" Then I went back inside and cried. My heroes were, after all, not invincible, but it made me sad to watch them defeated.

When they tore down my school a few years ago, a different sadness, whimsical and melancholy, came over me. The asphalt playground and the stone walls of Limestone Grade School were ploughed into rubble. I have a few pieces of demolished wall sitting on my back porch, mortar still stuck to the edges of the stone. In another now demolished building, the 1966 version of Busch Stadium in St. Louis, I saw a Cardinal hero and got his autograph. I never saw Stan Musial hit a baseball, except in grainy old videos. Dodgers Coach Ted Lyons once said that Mr. Musial "waits for a pitch in the unforgettable left-handed corkscrew crouch peering over his right shoulder looking like a kid peeking around the corner to see if the cops are coming." He was referred to by the Brooklyn Dodgers as simply, "The Man," a name that stuck, along with two statues outside Busch Stadium, one of which bears the words of former baseball commissioner Ford Frick, "Here stands baseball's perfect warrior. Here stands baseball's perfect knight." He was as transparent as Joe DiMaggio was mysterious, as elegant as Mickey Mantle was country, and as humble as Ted Williams was arrogant. Stan the Man signed my Rawlings baseball and handed it back with a sprawling blue autograph. The signature, "Stan Musial", was decipherable only because I watched the Man sign it across the table.

I lost that autographed ball, foolishly using it as an everyday ball in my backyard. It turned up years later, like an old friend, a memento of the time I was close enough to touch him and watch him scribble his name on my baseball. A buddy told me to put the ball in a safe place, but I didn't always take advice. I should have listened to the advice of a grizzled St. Louis concessionaire who sold me a hotdog at Busch Stadium when he admonished me to "Stick that five dollar bill in your pocket and quit waving it around!" I stared at him mouth agape, unsure of his meaning, and felt the friction of the currency leaving my hand, whereupon I turned to stare in disbelief at a boy my height and weight running up the ramp behind the row of concessions with my five bucks clenched in his fist. He stole my cash and my innocence.

That summer of 1969 was a summer of justice. A time to consider why a boy would steal my five bucks and how a pot-bellied southpaw like Mickey Lolich could beat my Cards three times in a World Series. I sought redemption for the Cards defeat in the 1968 World Series. Redemption through games played in my yard next to a driveway of gravel. My heroes, Lou Brock LF, Curt Flood CF, Roger Maris RF, Orlando Cepeda 1B, Tim McCarver C, Mike Shannon 3B, Julian Javier 2B, Dal Maxvill SS, Bob Gibson P, exceeded expectations on my yard in 1969, and they never lost a game to the Tigers all summer. I can still recite that lineup because I built a stadium in the backyard of my mind where these ballplayers came to practice their hitting, emerging from the oaks that surrounded our home like Shoeless Joe Jackson appearing out of a cornfield in a dream. That lineup of Cardinals spent the summer slugging gravel into the oak trees of our backyard using my wooden bat, a 30" Louisville Slugger autographed by Mickey Mantle and stamped by Hillerich and Bradsby. J.R.R. Tolkien said, "I am at home among trees." I too, was at home among trees, playing fantasy baseball alone in our yard, framed with oaks in a gentle arc. I imagined the trees as the outfield fence at Busch stadium in the evening gloaming, the shadows casting doubt on my reality and my fantasy. In my insular nine year-old universe of gravel baseball, I concocted World Series scenarios replete with standing room only crowds cheering lustily as they mingled with the oak trunks. I envisioned an elaborate game of rock hitting with metrics to assign singles (hard grounders into the trees), doubles (line drives into the lower trees) triples (line drives into the upper canopy, home runs (soaring shots clearing the tree tops) and outs (any swing and miss or dribbled grounder). In that manner I would bat through the Cards lineup mimicking each Cardinal, batting left handed for Brock, Maris, McCarver, and right handed for the rest of the lineup. I would pooch out my butt when Cepeda batted and flair the right elbow while standing erect when Flood hit, and deliberately hit a few weak grounders when Maxvill, barely a .200 hitter, was at the plate, although I once had him hit a home run late in a game just to improve his hitting morale.

After a summer of gravel baseball, somewhere deep within the gathering dusk of a late summer day, the head of the bat flew into the oak trees during an Orlando Cepeda plate appearance as the bat barrel could stand no more abuse, chiselled by the pounding of a nine year-old slamming one inch limestone aggregate deep into the trees, again and again, wood to woods. Before that final swing and goodbye to my Louisville Slugger, it looked like a beaver had taken a hungry bite from the meat of the bat head. Worn to a precarious sliver, it was gone.

I always knew my wooden bat from the summer of 1969 would die and things would never be the same again. Backyard games fade to oblivion as do our heroes, but our memories live on. I still recall fondly that bat with Mickey's signature burned in script on the barrel. That bat head flew into the trees along with Mickey Mantle's legacy as his life spiralled into addiction, partying coupled with the deterioration of his knees. As one writer put it, Mantle was "a million-dollar talent propped up on dime-store knees." This once fleet and nimble outfielder staggered under the towering fly ball of life against a blazing sun.

Musial and Mantle help me frame the scene that took place in the summer of 1969 at Busch Stadium. We were sitting on the third base side and I asked, "Dad, can I go get a hot dog?" Remarkably, he let me go alone. We lived in a safer world then, or perhaps we were simply oblivious to the Soviet ICBM's pointed at us, kids pedalling bikes without helmets, trailing the fog of DDT, safe in the assurance that a saccharine-laced Fresca washing down a nitrite infused hot dog was invigorating and healthy. At least I felt safe, until a street smart kid hit me in the gut and stole my five dollars and my innocence. I can still see that boy running up the ramp with five dollars clutched in his hand. I wonder where that kid is? Did his Dad take him to the ballgame and teach him how to hit, how to conduct himself, how to live? I knew nothing of his grief and pain, his joy and passion, his hunger and thirst. I've always wondered what he looked like viewed from the front.

The Man, the Mick and the Boy fought for what they wanted. A legacy of greatness...a streaking comet lifestyle...a five dollar bill. Next spring, I'll sit in the sun with the crowd and watch a ballgame. I'll eat a hotdog and think about how I miss the backyard ballpark where squirrels ran for cover that summer of 1969, dodging the rain of gravel as Cardinal hitters slammed stones deep into the leafy upper deck with a flawed legends bat. Mickey Mantle taught me about home runs but also about striking out and broken bat heads flying away. Stan the Man taught me about excellence, professional dignity, work ethic, and loyalty. And the boy? He's still teaching me.

Somewhere out there the boy is now a man. We share the same world and a five dollar bill and I hope he's stopped running. If I ever see him, I'll thank him. Not for stealing my five bucks, but for making me understand folks have passions and needs I can't understand. Boys who haven't found their wooden bat and a pile of gravel inside a leafy stadium. A place to swing like a hero, a place where you are no longer a boy, you are The Man, and you hit until your hands are blistered and your bat breaks in half and soars deep into the woods.

3

LBJ and Dad Lit The Fuse

On July 2, 1964, President Johnson signed into law the Civil Rights Act. Its enactment, following the longest continuous debate in the history of the U.S. Senate, enshrined into law the basic principle upon which our country was founded - that all people are created equal.

~ *Thomas Perez*

My favorite childhood holiday was the 4th of July. I had no precocious notions of patriotism, not one noble sentiment of love for country. I just loved fireworks. Sparklers, "please don't plunge them into the retina of your sister!", "Yes Mom, I'll be careful", and glow worms that mutated from fire to molten ebony marking our concrete driveway with a permanent trail of patriotism. Pop bottle rockets never saw the translucent glass of a bottle, only the finely-timed action of fleshy adolescent palms flinging the rocket on a stick into the smoky haze of summer evenings. My summers were punctuated with the report of Black Cats, Cherry Bombs and M-80's.

But my favorite firework was the Family Pack. There wasn't a fuse to light and it wasn't condoned by the Certified Firework Makers of America. It was the remainder, the bottom of the box, the leftovers of the Family Pack, when my Dad got tired of shooting them off one by one on a July 4th evening and he said, "Light 'em up." And we did. Roman candles, pop bottle rockets, Lady Fingers, and Whiz Bang Spinners, whatever we hadn't lit yet got lit, set on fire en mass. That was the culmination of our pyromania one summer evening in our Oklahoma backyard. It was memorable and colorful. And it was hard on the heels of some other fireworks.

The Civil Rights Act of 1964 and the Immigration Act of 1965 marked the year the Family Pack got lit all at once. Even as Lyndon Baines Johnson assured nervous Americans that the passage of the Immigration Act was not significant and "not a revolutionary bill. It does not affect the lives of millions…", he would tell us. And Ted Kennedy hastened to assure Americans that the demographic mix would not be changed. Really, Ted? Immigration law at the time of the passage excluded Latin Americans, Asians and Africans in quotas and preferred northern and western Europeans over southern and eastern Europeans.

In the volatile Sixties as I just began to understand that not all folks were white, something exploded, not just in our backyard, but in our collective national conscience. Had LBJ any sense that he had become like my Dad losing patience with lighting Lady Fingers one at a time? As he signed this Act into law at the foot of the Statue of Liberty, he unwittingly lit the Family Pack ablaze.

The notion of a melting pot where all cultures and colors create a kaleidoscope of thought, economic clout, creative energy, entertainment power and sports competitiveness is the world we live in today. It's the Family Pack exploded, tattooed, brilliant, participatory. We emerged from the shadowed halls of the pale skinned and crew cut, blinded by the light of diversity. The Celtics and the Packers were winning championships. High topped shoes with working class green and gold. Lombardi and Auerbach, Havlicek and Hornung, industrial packers and broad rimmed leprechauns dancing on fields and courts of established traditions, a white working class culture of sport and middle America.

But on the shoulders of Rosa Parks, Dr. Martin Luther King and many others, places like Atlanta and Memphis and Charlotte, became economically diverse international cities in the years following 1964, places with African-American mayors and sports stars. Atlanta's Fulton County Stadium was a project enabled by this diversity. The stadium was built and soon Henry Aaron came to town to play baseball in the deep south.

My memories of 1964 are simpler and whiter. I remember a teenage garage band a block away serenading the neighborhood on summer evenings trying to be the next Beach Boys or Beatles. I remember playing kick the can and whiffle ball and there was truth in the social sarcasm of The Monkees song, Another Pleasant Valley Sunday. It was the suburbs and charcoal was burning everywhere along with the haze of spent fireworks.

I remember playing basketball with the neighbor kids in our driveway and hearing the great sonic boom of jets flying over through the sound barrier. Space and the sky was the frontier and the United States of America, well, we were the cowboys. There wasn't anything our American ingenuity could not conquer. The sound barrier, the Soviet menace, the moon. Except perhaps the bullet from the rifle of Lee Harvey Oswald. And so as F. Scott Fitzgerald famously said at the end of The Great Gatsby, "... we beat on, boats against the current, borne back ceaselessly into the past."

Camelot came undone in 1964, our innocence ended, and we were borne back ceaselessly into the past. We were being borne back to the beginning of democracy, starting over, all in now. The colors exploded and we became a country of pastels and earth tones, warm colors and cool. It was during the summer of my early youth in the white-bread suburbs when the world was exploding that I watched my Dad light a Family Pack of fireworks, as the shutter was opened and the kaleidoscope of light spilled into my town, my country, my world.

Little did I understand about colors and cultures and races, but neither did LBJ, or my Dad. We were simply enjoying the fireworks during the summer our country burst forth into brilliance.

I've outgrown my love of fireworks. But I still love color and the freshness and life and vivid interest it brings into my world. A world filled with much more to eat than just hamburgers and potatoes, a world awash with the sound of much more to hear than the simple earthy English of the Midwest, a world with much more to see than brown-haired freckled faces, a world that challenges me to understand my place in it, to be proud of my heritage, proud of my country, proud of my family, even as I admire all the voices and faces and smells and foods and ways of those born far from the smoke of my own backyard.

4

The Color of God

We are never racist against somebody who is very far away. I don't know any racism against the Eskimos. To have a racist feeling, there must be another who is slightly different from us, but is living close to us.

~ *Umberto Eco*

The bus crossed the 7th street bridge and I peered over the rail through an open window at the eddies of a muddy river, swirling coffee relentlessly shaping the bank of naked earth. On my first day of junior high ringing bells punctuated my hourly class schedule, assaulting my senses along with the smells of lingering cigarette smoke in bathrooms, hot sawdust and oiled metal cuttings from shop class, the musty sour odor of the gym class unwashed, and the siren smell of shampooed hair - the same hair that framed stick figure girls in grade school now bent beautiful by the refraction of our hormones and youthful vision, those same linear girls now inhabiting the curved bodies of mystic goddesses.

Junior high was loud and the noise drove me to quiet corners like a puppy hearing the roar of constant chatter in the halls, the din of the gorgeous set against the quietness of those not, a dissonance heard only by the muted introverts. Gym teachers yelled, music teachers coaxed, and math teachers factored while the whispers of the popular determined the fate of the not, along with something similar, ancient but newly strange... *racism*. This was my first round in the boxing ring, a toe-to-toe match with the colorful tapestry of peers that would one day become a coat of many colors.

I came from an all-white grade school into a place that exploded my world of sameness, milling hallways filled with kids of color and culture. I began my education at Central Junior High understanding how different I was, that I wasn't normal, that I was indeed the odd one because of how little I knew about the beliefs, traditions, myths and stories of people who didn't look like me, who didn't sound like me. And amazingly, my new friends didn't even play basketball like me.

I was hidden under a white wicker basket in a cloistered and wooded haven, happy in my oblivious suburb, not unlike the canopied Caney river dividing our town into an east and west side as it flowed indifferently towards the Gulf of Mexico. This unhurried river, hidden by oak and elm, flowed like warm caramel along the path of least resistance, seduced by gravity and an ever fattening burden of silt, a mirror of my flowing subconscious, silent truth cutting great banks of earth and changing course unaware. As I crossed over the Caney, I became aware of the river separating me, a wonder bread kid from the east side, and my friend, Walter, who lived across the river on the west side, a million miles away.

My latent blindness was as innocent as my Grandma's as she read her Bible, prayed, went to Africa on a mission trip…and in blind moments of remarkable relief set against my filter of appropriateness… used the "N" word. She did it without any hint of malice, although my innocence mistook her condescension for affection. She was a very kind-hearted woman, so I don't judge her. But I had seen black folk on television, and thought them to be normal, even heroic. I watched Sidney Poitier in *The Lilies of the Field*, Cassius Clay standing over Sonny Liston, and Jim Brown in a Cleveland Brown's uniform (I thought they named the team for him instead of Paul) running with a football and a satchel of grenades in an army uniform sprinting to his heroic death in the movie, *The Dirty Dozen*.

I had no idea blacks could hate blacks and whites could hate whites, as I sang "Jesus Loves the Little Children" in Sunday school. I did not yet understand the array of rich but lighter colored ethnicity baked into the bagels and ciabattas and ryes and sourdough of America's cultural oven. I hadn't seen *The Godfather* yet, with the opening scenes of the wedding party which would come to remind me of the Italians I met when I lived in South Jersey twenty years later, as I suddenly became the white minority and Italians, Jews, Irish and Jersey Pineys made fun of my slow Midwest accent and asked me about the Indians in Oklahoma. Nor had I discovered white on white bigotry in my own backyard, a festering socioeconomic hatred framed poetically by S.E. Hinton in *The Outsiders*, a world sharply divided by grease and shampoo. I was culturally snow blind in the womb of my Midwestern cocoon of sameness.

I walked close to the walls of Central Junior High. I kept my head down, stayed away from those who were different. I wasn't hostile or socially dull, just underexposed to culture other than my own. My integration had thus far been limited to my television set, seminal moments, mostly athletic and involving African-Americans, such as the Black Power salute. Tommy Smith raising a black gloved right fist and John Carlos raising his left gloved fist, standing on the award pedestal after finishing 1st and 3rd respectively in the two hundred meter dash at the Olympic Games in October of 1968. I once sensed defiance in pictures of Tommy Smith and John Carlos. Now I understand defiant posture as a plea for justice, the animation of prayer in the oppressed: Two men standing together with a white sprinter from Australia named Peter, asking God to set right the world, a world inhabited by red, yellow, black and white, a world that presented a gold medal to Tommy Smith but told him he was excluded from certain hotels and restaurants, country clubs, and conversations.

There is a grand tradition of fists raised in the name of justice, some might even name it wrestling with God, times where prayer is more of a dialogue rather than monologue, spirited debating with God Almighty: Abraham questioned God's promise and his own virility; Moses argued incompetence and asked God to send a more eloquent man to Pharaoh; Job ranted; David's mouth grew parched calling for help; Jacob transformed wrestling with someone you love into an art form by calling on God to bless him before he was beaten to a pulp.

As time goes by, I think of prayer with progressively bigger shoulders, throwing an occasional punch, less a mental exercise, more sweat and heavy lifting, a spirit in motion, gulping raw eggs with Rocky and running the steps of the Philadelphia Museum of Arts, like Tommy Smith and John Carlos raising gloved fists. In the United States of America, African-Americans have prayed for many years with emotion, prayed with faith, prayed with belief that someday life will be better and not just better, just.

And so I think of the journey beginning with my exposure to people of a different color and culture at my junior high school in 1971, which brought me to my senses and extinguished my hope of playing NBA basketball. Walter and I loved basketball. We found friendship playing ball, although we lived on opposite sides of the river and chiseled our places in the pecking order of junior high school culture using unique forms of power and leverage steeped in the tradition each of us knew. This constant social tension was unspoken but real. Sometimes punches were thrown, some malicious, some unintentional, both often landed. My front upper left tooth was chipped courtesy of a shadow boxing match gone awry between Walter and me. It was our freshman year and we were in the locker room being fourteen year old boys, feigning machismo, seeking affirmation, something or someone to tell us we were men.

Strength was the measuring stick, the mark of dominance. I saw gloveless boxing, fighting in the halls, black on white, white versus white, black on black, bare knuckles, playground fighting, slamming one another into lockers over the trivialities that kids often fought over. It was the accepted dueling method rather than pistols at twenty paces. Only Walter and me weren't really fighting, just horsing around. He could have slammed dunked me and mopped the tile floors shiny with my raggedy head. No, it was more like a big brother patronizing a younger, letting him get in a blow, shadow boxing playfully, just throwing punches with the intent of saying I could take you if I wanted, but not really wanting to hurt you. Except he miscalculated and busted my tooth.

Walter was the best athlete I knew. During the winter of our ninth grade year, I watched from the bench as Walter and Mike and Myron and Ricky, all African-American kids along with a white Catholic kid named Chet, led a team of otherwise short white guys to a rousing basketball win over our cross-town rival across the river, the all-white team that hadn't been beaten in their entire three-year junior high career.

That was a surreal moment for me as I thought we had no chance to win. I never really thought about those four African-American starters, about how it made them feel, how it may have empowered them, helped them become stronger in a world still dominated by white teachers and coaches and principals and mayors and governors and presidents. Perhaps this tension was unspoken but visceral, resulting in many wildly thrown punches at something unseen, undefined, not yet born in our social consciousness. We were trying to understand this shift in attitudes which started with the Emancipation Proclamation by President Lincoln on January 1, 1863 and traveled a bloody and bitter battle along back roads of hatred and ignorance, through the Supreme Court and Brown vs. Brown, and through the armed force of the National Guard at Central High School in Little Rock.

And it came down to a white kid with a chipped tooth swinging wildly at a black kid who could kick my butt. I hadn't heard Martin Luther King, Jr.'s I Have a Dream Speech. I didn't know much of letting freedom ring. I was just trying to get along as best I could. But I did know that the world in which I had been introduced left me uncertain, timid, unsure. The basketball court, however, was the place of refuge for me and for kids of all color, the place we lost our fear and found our competitive pride and spirit. For many of us who defined each other by sport, a basketball court was where we found freedoms ring.

Not long after the Civil Rights Act of 1964 and the 1966 NCAA National Championship game when Texas Western beat an all-white Kentucky basketball team, I was introduced to the freeing of the spirit of black America. The trail of struggle and history spilled out into our world, our playgrounds and locker rooms, our athletic fields and stages, our hallways and classrooms. We were kids struggling to enflesh the framework of laws decreed by our government that transformed our junior high from a place of Constitutional theory to one of practical action, made vibrant and colorful by the idea that all men and women are created equal.

I don't really think of those days as the "good old days". They were difficult, awkward, we didn't even know we were punching and ducking. We were, in fact, living out the words of the old Negro spiritual reconstituted by U2, *I Still Haven't Found What I'm Looking For*, believing in a Kingdom where all the colors bleed into one, but not knowing how, except to get into the ring and spar with sweat, blood, and color spilled on the canvas.

James McBride was the son of a black father and a white Jewish mother. When he was young, he asked his mother about her being different. She would simply say 'I'm light skinned.' Then he began to think himself different and asked his mother if he was black or white. 'You're a human being,' she replied. Then James asked her, "What color is God?" For years he asked this question and his mother declined to answer. Finally, one day he asked and she told him, "God is the color of water."

Ron Williams, Brent Taylor, Scott Stuart, Walter Reece, Kevan Mueller.

Some days I'm reminded of the surreal nature of this earth and that I'm a stranger in a strange land. I'm grateful for those awkward days of youth and thankful for a slightly broken smile that reminds me of the way it used to be when we shadow boxed one another in the halls of our school bobbing and weaving and swinging, challenged to understand what it meant to live in a world of red and yellow and black and white, in a Kingdom where all the colors are bleeding into one, in a Universe created by a God who is for all I know, the color of water.

5

The Man from 1933

I imagine people I admire, when they were young. What were they like in their prime, before I existed? This story is about one of those moments imagining people who have walked before me, often in the same pastures.

~ brent taylor

I walked through my front door this morning and was startled by the dense mechanical ring of the oak & metal Bell Telephone Company phone mounted on the wall of our living room facing out to the east garden. I had never heard it ring before since it's only an antique, so my curiosity piqued, I ambled over and gingerly lifted the ancient earpiece. "Hello", I mumbled tentatively into the black spout mouthpiece. "Hi," replied the man on the other end. "I was calling to ask about the cattle you have to sell. I'm looking to buy." Stunned by the voice coming from the old wooden box with no wired connection (had antique phones entered the cell era through a warping of time and space?), I wondered while pondering what to say to this would-be cattle buyer.

"I need to buy a Hereford breeder to add to our herd. Can I come by and take a peek at your cows?" My reply was otherworldly, from someplace other than my consciousness. "You betcha, c'mon out." The flinty response was immediate and sounded eerily familiar, "Be there in an hour." I wandered out to the front porch after a spell and sat on the mahogany swing and waited, kick flexing my left knee out and in, listening to the crackle of 53-year-old cartilage, while pushing back with my right foot and lifting it slightly to let the swing descend, wobbling forward like a kid's first bike ride.

From the north came the clatter of a 1931 Four-cylinder Ford Model A flatbed truck lurching along the asphalt toward my house. Round headlamps earnestly pressing forward followed by the box cab and black-visored windshield, and a flatbed enclosed with a triple rail wood sideboard. The distinct saucer headlamps looked like eyeglasses and the windshield visor, along with the clattering made me think of a near-sighted bookkeeper rolling along on vulcanized rubber wheels. I watched him climb out of the truck and walk toward me, 6'1", dark hair slightly receding, sun-worn smile creases forever marking him as a friendly man. He wore overalls and a white t-shirt, weathered-round toe work boots, and he moved along the ground as if he were part of the earth, like he owned a farm or had a garden. "Afternoon. Are you Taylor?" the man drawled in an easy and unaffected way. I replied, "Yes sir. Ya come to see the herd?" It occurred to me that I did not own any cows, but these words flowed from my lips from places I had seen but never been, like honey dripping off a ladle.

As we walked toward the herd, crossing the cattle guard up and over the berm next to the pond, I asked, "Where ya from?" "The Oklahoma Panhandle," he replied. "I'm on my way to Arkansas. If we can strike a deal, I'll stop on my way back and make arrangements to pick up the breeder." To which I replied, "Just take your time and pick out what suits you." And I watched him pacing along the edge of the herd, eyeing several of the smaller bulls. I thought that he looked like Tom Joad in the Grapes of Wrath as I watched him make his choice. Afterwards, walking back up to the house, I asked if he had family. "I do, just had a baby girl, name is Jessie." We strolled along and he talked about being a Dad, how having a daughter had changed him in ways he never anticipated, how the world was changing so quickly, and he spoke of losing their wheat crop to the drought, everything withering in the hot blowing dust, wondering how he would ever support his wife and baby daughter. I stole a glance at him as he talked and he seemed wise in a way I couldn't quite comprehend, like he knew my story, even though he seemed to be twenty years younger than me.

My cell phone rang. It was my wife. I hung up and he looked at me, then at my phone. "What is that?" I looked down at my I phone 5 and told him it's a phone…without the wires. The signal goes through the air. And you can get online, check email and the social media and…" I recognized the blank stare as lack of comprehension. And so I just told him, "It's how we run our lives now, how we talk to each other, how we communicate." I asked him, "So where you live you don't have these?" "No," came the reply. "What is your technology?" I asked him. He replied, "Hard work, desperation, hope, faith, failure, not knowing how we'll make it another day…that's how we get by…just know somehow we will." Then he said something I'll never forget. "Can your five phone tell you why I get up every day before the sun rises? Or tell me why I'm here? Tell me what's important? Can it tell me why I love my baby daughter so? What causes greatness? What causes failure? Happiness? Can it tell me what my life will be like in ten years? Twenty? Forty?" As the young man drove away I looked down at my phone and in my other hand five silver dollars he had handed me for a deposit on the Hereford. There was an eagle on the back and a woman in a spiked crown on the front. The words "Liberty" arched over the top edge of the coins along with the banner phrase on one line, "In God We Trust." They were vintage 1921 coins. I slipped them into my pocket and walked back into my house through the front door.

Weary, I went to my recliner and extended it fully, closing my eyes. I awoke an hour later and remembered the time last month I walked through the cemetery north of town, looking down at my Grandpa Jess grave, with the important stuff chiseled on the face, born 1901- died 1969. I knew him only the last ten years of his life. I walked into my closet and pulled open the top sock drawer. That's where I keep important stuff because it seems safe and I can see it every day. Nestled near the back of the drawer next to my 1979 U.S. Amateur pin, was a quarter my Grandpa gave me in 1968 when he picked me up at school and asked me to help him. I rode with him over in his Ford truck to Woodland Park where he was working on a house. He said, "Can you stick your arm into that hole in the wall and pull out that wire?" I told him sure. But after trying for several minutes, I gave up. I had failed.

He drove me home and as I was getting out of the truck, he reached into his pocket and pulled out a quarter, handed it to me and said, "Thanks." I walked to the porch and sat down, watching my Grandpa drive away. I glanced down at the worn Washington quarter and read the top word gently arching along the coin edge, "Liberty", and clustered to one side "In God We Trust." The year embossed along the bottom, 1933.

6

Discovering the Holy Among the Profane in Fifteen Minutes

When my spiritual strength begins to fail, I know a remedy, I will go to the table of the Lord; there will I drink and recover my decayed strength.

~ *Bernard of Clairvaux*

I grew up in a home that severely limited my creative outlet of language. I wasn't allowed to curse, nor was I given the freedom to vent with words that hinted of the real four-letter curse words, the baby curse words like "heck" and "shoot" and "darn." These were deemed unpolished and tainted by the very notion of adjacency, they contained at least two of the evil four letters. I don't remember many lectures from Mom, the language gatekeeper, but there was instilled in our vocabulary a maternal conscience which filtered the borderline words readily when Mom was in the room, and a little less severely when we were playing outside.

I was reminded of this by an email from my cousin, Mark Davis, who in the midst of lecturing one of his children caught in the act of euphemistic common language, flashed back to moments in his childhood when his expressive euphemistic wings had been clipped by the keeper of holiness in our home. He wasn't remembering this painfully as one remembers getting whacked like a piñata Jedi style with a wooden stick by a penguin like the Blues Brothers endured as they sat in grammar school unidesks. No, this was a grateful wistfulness with which Mark wrote about his Aunt Charlotte who taught her unruly children and nephews as we tested the airwaves of the profane.

At the end of the email, Mark asked this question. "What's the meaning of Matthew 25: 1-13. What does it mean to be ready? What does the oil represent?"

Just before Jesus trial and crucifixion, he tells three stories recorded in Matthew 25, all of which relate to being ready. The first is a story about ten bridesmaids, five of whom are prepared with oil and five who are not. But they all have lamps and they all fall asleep and all awake to a groom coming down the street and as they prepare to enter the wedding party, the five without oil are turned away to go acquire more oil.

Matthew 25:11: Later the others also came. "Lord, Lord," they said, "open the door for us!" But he replied, "Truly I tell you, I don't know you."

Cousins and brothers replied with more questions, perhaps the oil is knowledge, maybe the oil is the Spirit of God or salvation, maybe it's just olive oil? I have a good friend who worships in a different church than me, and we have an ongoing discussion about church and faith. I asked him why they enjoy the Lord's Supper seasonally and he asked me why we observe it weekly. I thought I knew the answer, but maybe my friend was correct to apply the 'less is more' principle. But, I wonder if weekly observance of faith, the liturgy of wine and bread, is related to the question of storing oil in my lamp?

A lamp in the ancient world provided light for celebrations, like wedding parties which often lasted into the evening hours. Light was required and lamps or torches provided a certain amount of expendable light. This light was extinguished once the olive oil was exhausted.

Civilization progressed from torches to lamps fueled by olive oil to street lamps burning whale oil and petroleum oil, from filament bulbs to fluorescent to halogen to led lights. Our world is lit with little thought about replacing an led bulb for ten thousand hours. Unthinkable to the ancient holder of the lamp who constantly stopped to replenish oil and trim the chard of the wick every fifteen minutes.

The Lord's Supper or Communion, is a time to leave behind the profane because there is room for nothing else. What we do around the table of communion is about the intersection of our earth-bound commonness and our Redeemer who says come, eat and drink with me in a place and moment of remarkable distinction from our humanity.

Here is an amazing idea. There is only one dispenser of grace in the entire universe. Grace can't be learned in education, acquired online at Amazon, fought for in athletic competition, earned at work, grace can't mandated by government, doled out through welfare, grace isn't passed along by human birthright. The only place we can fill our lamp is Christ's body and in his Church and around a table.

Perhaps God sees us running around like ants at a picnic marching in furiously paced to and fro lines of constant activity, we're all doing the same thing, the human thing, our legs are churning, our arms are carrying, not speaking much about anything real, not concerned about running out of oil, marching one by one to our next morsel of food not bothering to check our fuel gauge... but we sit down in a room together and just for a moment...the profane touches the holy...earth intersects with heaven.. we remember how much our we are loved...and the oil gauge needle ticks up a notch. And so a bit of flat bread reminds us of Christ's body becomes our mission and we drink juice from a vine that reminds us of blood and our redemption and of grace. We put these into our mouths and we marvel at God rescuing us from our own perverse sense that we can save ourselves somehow at the pump of self-righteousness.

This earth is filled with so much heartache, brokenness, planes disappear from radar, we strive, we work, we go to weddings, we go to funerals...but this moment of overlap between the profane and the holy is one that God says we share, where our sodden wanderings touch the majestic and perhaps if we are still enough we'll feel God coming along and touch us on the elbow and say "I hope you had a good week, it's good to hear your voice, I love you...thanks for remembering me." And we eat and we drink and we are filled with the stuff of grace and our spirits are filled with the inspiration of a Savior who loved us with tenacious gentleness and amazing grace.

The Lord's Supper nourishes grace, which like a lamp, is apt to go out if not often fed with oil, and it's not stored in LED lamps that burn for ten thousand hours, but sustained in the constant contact of an intimate God who lives and speaks and listens to us in fifteen minute bits of holiness. One day our lamps will never go out, but for now I'm reminded of the constancy of the fountain of restoration where I can go and set aside my ant hill of living and speak to the transcendent everlasting who lights the world with ten thousand LED lights on a thousand hills. And I choose one hill among the thousand to set my fifteen minute lamp next to those eternal lights and marvel at the brilliance.

7

Walking in Green Pastures

Golf is the cruellest game, because eventually it will drag you out in front of the whole school, take your lunch money and slap you around.

~ Rick Reilly, "Master Strokes," Sports Illustrated

I played professional golf long enough to have a cup of coffee with Fred Couples, Mark O'Meara and Hal Sutton, and if I smoked, a pack of cigarettes with John Daly. I played with John in the Arkansas Amateur as he flicked his cigarette to the ground before playing a shot, then immediately picked up the cigarette like a forlorn lover, tenderly sparking passion in reunion as a burning ember released a toxic cloud on a velvet fairway. This was golf without conscious played in the midst of addiction. Young John Daly played with little intention, easily distracted, like the round of golf was interrupting his smoke break. I'm easily the least famous of this group and proud of that fact. I'm an introvert and if not for the encouragement of a Gospel preacher named Sidney Roper, I could never have teed up the ball on the 1st hole against players of that ability.

The tee shot at the opening hole is the most difficult shot in tournament golf. Playing partners, the starter, the gallery, all eyes fixed on that first shot, the swing that breaks loose the tension and releases the pressure, breathtaking silence roaring like the ocean in seashells, mingled with slippery thoughts of bad things that might happen. The golfer dissolves into a cloud of degenerate self-talk, 'Just don't whiff it, get it down there somewhere, keep it on the golf course, don't hit someone in the gallery.' It's a moment of faith in which you are all alone without a teammate.

My biggest 1st tee failures happened at the United States Amateur in Cleveland, Ohio in 1979. I was born twenty years earlier in July of 1959, and my family attended the Sixth and Dewey Church of Christ where Sidney Roper was not only my first image of a preacher, but also my first picture of a golf ambassador, a man who walked in green pastures and wore the shoes of a fisherman. His polished black wing tip shoes skipped along church house floors and caressed the green pastures of a church without walls. He walked a golf course with the intention that Mr. Daly had misplaced, walking like he had an airport conveyor belt under his winged feet. His brand of golf was a swift walk in the park accompanied by the graceful swing of a shepherds crook. I stared at the shoes of the preacher, at those wing tips, rather than at his eyes because the shoes were closer to my vision and I found the dimple pattern mesmerizing, more elaborate than the dimples of a golf ball, curved, hypnotic, elegant, dimpled shoes.

Besides, it was easier to look down at the shoes of royalty. Mr. Roper had an inside track to the throne room and at the age of three, I feared the powerful, and those to whom everyone flocked for encouragement. The preacher man looked down at my three-year-old shaved head, and this unapproachable adult righteousness that I feared, this holy fame, everyone lined up to speak to him after sermons, his ceaseless energy, was beyond my understanding of sociological affirmation. So I skirted the sermon greeting line running outside to climb on the ledge next to the block windows. Yet he persisted, he pursued me, even though I was just a kid.

But as a kid, he not only included me, he welcomed me, into a familiar sanctuary. With a club under my arm I followed Sidney and my Dad around the golf course where I learned the game and I also learned things like hole every putt, challenge yourself by playing from the professional tees, and Sidney taught me how to put a whole bag of Planter's peanuts into a Coca-Cola slurping it all in one step, fuel and fire, his game and vigor fanned by the chemistry of Coke and peanuts.

I was the best young golfer he'd seen although I didn't believe his assessment listening mutely to his praise. It wasn't long before I beat this man who could hit a Titleist out of sight and he loved it and continued with encouragement, "You should try out for the U.S. Amateur." I was only twelve years old so I said maybe next year. Every year he'd say "You should try out for the U.S. Amateur" and he'd tell me about growing up in Texas, caddying for spending money and when I made it to the U.S. Amateur, he would be my caddy. The summer of my fourteenth birthday, I shot a 74 and began to believe. Maybe I could play in the U.S. Amateur.

At the age of nineteen, I entered the 1979 U.S. Amateur and played a qualifier against other college golfers and amateurs at Southern Hills Country Club and I qualified for the 1979 National Amateur. We loaded into a Winnebago the following week, Mom, Dad and family friend, George Johnson, and Sidney and Sue Roper, and we traveled to Cleveland, Ohio and Canterbury Country Club. I walked in to register at the Canterbury Club and a man took me to the locker room and showed me where I could change shoes and assigned my locker and he asked me to sign the U.S. Amateur program that had my name on it, my first autograph. He said, "You never know who'll be famous someday, so I ask every participant to sign my program."

I never became famous, but many in that field did, John Cook, Mark O'Meara, Hal Sutton, all players who would go on to compete on the PGA Tour and win several of golf's Major Titles. I sat on my hotel bed the night before the opening round and read about a golfer from Shreveport named Hal Sutton who had already won the Western Amateur that summer. I was playing *with* Hal Sutton who would win the PGA Championship in 1983 and captain the Ryder Cup team later in his career. On the biggest stage in amateur golf I was playing with one of the best amateur golfers in the world.

The first hole at Canterbury Country Club in Cleveland is a par four dogleg right that demands a power fade to follow the shape and contour of the fairway. George Johnson caddied for me that day and he handed me the driver, a laminated Power-Bilt with a titanium shaft. I teed my Titleist and ripped it straight down the left edge of the fairway but the ball flew rifle straight and bounced through the fairway into the left rough. A man in the gallery behind me exclaimed, "He didn't cut it." To which my Mom, taking offence and not knowing the subtleties of maneuvering a tee shot on a U.S.G.A. course set for the Amateur or of golf shot commentary and terminology, replied, "That was a gooooood shot." Thank you Mom, but I knew. He was right. I didn't cut it enough. The ball was in deep U.S.G.A. rough and I gouged it out with an 8 iron, then chipped past the cup to 30 feet and drained that long putt for par. I shot 78 with bogeys on the last three holes. Distraught, disappointed, I realized my chances of shooting a number in the sixties the next day to reach the round of match play were slim.

The second round was just down the road at Shaker Heights Country Club and Sidney caddied for me. Sidney was filled with enthusiasm and couldn't wait to get started caddying in the U.S. Amateur and even though I had a disappointing first day he was excited, he believed I could come back and play well the second day.

Sidney handed me my driver and hustled down the 1st tee box to the landing area 280 yards out and stationed himself in the trees. Hal hit first and smoked his drive 290 yards center cut in the middle of the fairway. Then Sidney, fidgeting behind a giant maple tree, watched as I swung hard and barely caught a piece of the ball. It may have been the worst shot I've ever hit. Sidney craned his neck looking but never saw a ball because it simply dribbled off the tee 30 yards into the thick grass in front of the tee box. I walked that short walk like it was my last walk, slowly, head down, embarrassed. I sheepishly waved at him to come back with my clubs. I shot 74 that day. It wasn't good enough, but Sidney never lost faith in me. He is one of the reasons I never quit or give up. He taught me to dream big dreams and to not only be a person of faith, but to believe in other people.

I eventually got over my disappointment. Two years later, I finished tied for 5th in the National Collegiate NAIA tournament and was named to the All-America Team. Success at competitive levels is about believing. Belief in hard work, belief in your skills, belief in fair play, and belief that what you do is meaningful. Sidney taught me those things through the game of golf, walking along green pastures with purpose, with intention, with passion and belief.

I think about how he abided in faith and believed. He believed in an unimaginably wonderful and gracious and boundless Creator. And not only did he abide in the holy sense of God and Church, Sidney abounded in the world, always taking interest in the hearts and souls of those he touched. He was proud of me, no matter how far he had to retrace his steps on the first hole of the U.S. Amateur in 1979.

Sidney died in October of 2011 at the age of 92. His oldest son, Sidney Roper Jr. called me and asked if I would lead singing at Sidney's funeral. I told him that it would be an honor. At the funeral service, I told about how he taught me to lead the song *Abide With Me* and we sang it together. Sidney not only abided in those wing tip shoes fishing for souls, he abounded in green pastures swinging a golf club with grace and passion.

Sidney was 59 years of age when he caddied for me in Cleveland. It never seemed odd to him to pick up the bag of a 19-year old and lug it around a golf course raking sand traps and tending flags and replacing divots. He did it naturally with grace and class. Sidney is one of my heroes in that great cloud of witness, a faithful man who believed, an encourager who made me a better man.

Sidney putted out every putt, walked every fairway, played the pro tees when he didn't have to, and when he did have to, he turned around and walked back to the 1st tee box because his golfer needed him. To paraphrase the Psalmist, the Epistle of John and the Hebrew letter, "The Lord is my shepherd, I shall not want. He makes me to lie down in green pastures; He restores my soul; He leads me in the paths of righteousness , for His name's sake...but if we walk in green pastures, we experience a green pasture with one another, even in those moments we can't drive the ball off a tee box in moments of pressure...for God had a better plan for us, that their faith and our faith would come together to make one completed whole, their lives of faith not complete apart from ours."

8

Fill Up the Back of that Shovel Son

Working hard and working smart sometimes can be two different things.

~ Byron Dorgan

"Build a better mousetrap and the world will beat a path to your door" is a phrase I learned in a Harding University marketing class. The phrase originated with Ralph Waldo Emerson although Mr. Emerson's original statement was a bit different. "If a man has good corn or wood or boards or pigs to sell, or can make better chairs or knives, crucibles or church organs, than anybody else, you will find a broad hard-beaten road to his house, though it be in the woods." In 1889 the modern mousetrap was created and patented. Though Emerson had died seven years previous, Emerson was quoted as saying: "If a man can write a better book, preach a better sermon, or make a better mousetrap than his neighbor..."

As a teenager working in the family homebuilding business, Grandpa Taylor told me, "Fill up the back of the shovel and the front will take care of itself." My shovel work at nineteen was marked by wild and raw energy, which peaked during the heat wave of 1980 while we were working a foundation on a sun-baked hilltop. The sandy loam flew out of the ditch, slung without discretion, a blast furnace summer mingled with Oklahoma dust caking our blushed skin, sweat sprouting from brow, leaking down our faces, like copper rivers flowing down our neck and brown tributaries mapping shirtless torso. My buddy Jeff and I shovelled in grimy solidarity, hot shovels shining like sabres in the stilting oppression that tinged the grass the color of toast. We were the ditch scrapers, followers of the clawed beast, a canary yellow Case backhoe. We slung dirt clods like bad elves flinging hard candy at a Christmas parade, keepers of the ditch, clean and square. We owned that ditch.

Paul Newman made sport of chain-gang labor along a Dixie road in the movie *Cool Hand Luke*. Newman's character, Luke, rallies his fellow prisoners to a frenetic pace, slinging gravel screenings atop fresh tar.

With hours of daylight remaining and the road work complete, the inmates realize the implications of their astonishing burst of speed, and the guards, attune to the inmates sense of camaraderie, ready their weapons awaiting an insurrection, unclear of the meaning of their furious effort. "Have you seen Cool Hand Luke and the chain gang scene with inmates scattering gravel on hot tar?" I said to Jeff. He replied, "Yep, what about it?" I told him, "Why don't we get this done, and head for the shade of that oak?" And we did. We flung dirt with magnificent obsession, our faces gleaming with sweat and inspiration. Motivated only by an early finish and the relief of a spreading oak tree, we made shovel speed history. Why will inmates forced to work and nineteen year old college kids earning five dollars an hour risk heat stroke with the only tangible incentive being knocking off early?

Grandpa Taylor believed in working easy, not hard. He was in the furniture business and drove a Wonder bread truck and later joined my Dad in the home building business. Grandpa learned the easiest way to complete a task, an ergonomical analyst in a straw Stetson and boots, never pushing too hard, bending at the knees, lifting with the core, and sweating only when necessary.

Benjamin Franklin said, "Dost thou love life? Then do not squander time, for that's the stuff life is made of." Legendary UCLA basketball coach John Wooden advised his players to "Be quick but don't hurry." Wooden believed that hurry is an emotional state that breeds bad decisions, but quickness is a learned skill acquired by physical and mental training. We live with a continual tension between creative perfection and furious haste understanding *we don't always have time to do our best*.

At the age of sixteen, I drove a 1970 International dump truck while cleaning houses for my Dad, filling the truck bed at job sites and driving across the Cherokee bridge to the landfill. I tested the limits of the truck in each gear like an Indy car driver on a Sunday. Returning from the dump one morning, I pulled up to the curb next to the house we were building, a house I would later live in and a house my son now calls his first home. Grandpa stood on the front porch waiting on me. "Sit down, I need to talk to you," he said. And I sat on the step and listened to Grandpa Ross. "Slow down," and "Don't goose the engine," and "Understand the power of what is underneath you," and "I'm disappointed in you."

I still remember the weight of that disappointment. Perhaps that rebuke instilled the seed of a greater spirit of creativity nurtured in the spirit of unhurried work.

My three-year-old son sat on the same front step with me, twenty years later, listening to a lecture about speed and control and wild things. I sent him into the house properly chastised and it dawned on me that I sat on this same step with Grandpa Ross twenty years ago. I got up slowly and followed Brandon into the house, thinking about how life comes around, beautifully, unhurried. You fall asleep and then awake, and realize you are standing in a man's boots, telling your son to slow down, don't goose the engine, tomorrow will be here soon enough.

I don't shovel so furiously these days. I'm more like Coach Wooden and Grandpa Ross, quick but not hurried, my pace measured by the back of a shovel.

9

Shooting Guns and Buttering Corn with the NRA

The romantic love we feel toward the opposite sex is probably one extra help from God to bring you together, but that's it. All the rest of it, the true love, is the test.

~ *Joan Chen*

My wife reminds me occasionally that I forgot to propose, and that our marriage certificate was not notarized properly under the laws of New Jersey. We've been not married for 29 years now. To assuage my guilt, awash in the glut of new age engagements initiated by princes in hot air balloons accompanied by life-sized stuffed giraffes, I'm finding new ways to say I love you to my love.

Here's one, prompted by her absence for a week as she travelled to spend time with our daughters. You had me at hello…woops…that was for Zellweger, although Karen loves Tom Cruise. Seriously, being single for a week makes me realize how lucky I am. Furthermore, bachelorhood confirms my helpless nature and the inverse of the Tom Cruise statement, "Your absence, my aloneness, incompletes me." How romantic.

The gaping void also magnifies my sense that whatever weirdness inhabits my soul grows exponentially in the vacuum of singularity. For instance, tonight I bought a gun and four kinds of corn and I hung out with the NRA crowd.

It started one morning when I discovered more holes in my yard than in the dried bed of Camp Green Lake. I had spotted the culprit, an armadillo, a few months ago. When I mentioned this to my friend Jim, he said, "Shoot it dead." "But I don't own a gun," I replied. "Ya gotta kill it or it will take over your lawn, eat your corn and drive your John Deere while you sleep."

Since the pantry was bare and my house was gunless, I headed off to Bass Pro Shop. I decided to buy a pellet gun, since it looked like if you bought a real gun they would take you to an interrogation room with one way glass heated by klieg lights, strap you to a lie detector and ask if you really had the skill, experience and savvy to buy a real gun. I felt under-qualified in the bright lights of the NRA crowd. I paid for the lesser gun, a package of .177 pellets and several co2 cartridges and gingerly walked out the door into the view of a uniformed young man. I first thought he was a Marine with questions about my gun, but he turned out to be a boy scout selling popcorn so I bought twenty dollars of Extra Buttery Roasted Summer Corn (it tastes like corn on the cob).

Then I drove to the other NRA crowd, the nuts, raisins, and apples crowd at Sprouts grocery, and hung with them awhile. I love that place just like I love Bass Pro Shop. I'm not certain I fit in with either NRA crowd. One NRA wants to shoot, catch, and trap everything before eating or stuffing it, and the other NRA wants to save, sustain, nurture, then eat it and tell everyone else to stuff it. Both NRA's want to get at stuff and eat it, they just go about it with different tools. I bought all the corn I could and drove home.

After 29 years and another weekend alone, it's time to propose: Karen, I love you, marry me, and come home soon. I'm tired of eating corn and hanging out with the NRA.

10

That Which Burns Inwardly and Sears the Soul

"Phil is brilliant, but he's nuts. There's something not quite right about that boy. Phil is watching a movie that only Phil can see. His mother told me, 'Phil was so clumsy as a little boy, we had to put a football helmet on him until he was 4 because he kept bumping into things.' I told her, 'Mary, Mary, I'm a writer, you can't keep handing me material like this.' So the next time I saw Phil I said, 'You didn't really wear a football helmet in the house until you were 4, did you?' He said, 'It was more like 5.'"

David Feherty describing the competitive nature of golfer Phil Mickelson

David Feherty describing how Phil Mickelson behaves while playing golf, like a "drunk chasing a balloon near a cliff," reminds me that I suffer from the same malady, an unmistakable fingerprint of my personality imposed upon my golf game. And it reminds me that I've always been burdened by the cumbersome baggage of my addiction to golf.

Once while standing on a hill in Ardmore, Oklahoma some years ago, I decided to visit the grave of a man whom I have always loved...and hated.

Perry Duke Maxwell lay buried two hundred yards from where I stood, waiting to hit a seven-iron from one of Maxwell's famous elevated tee boxes at Dornick Hills Country Club. I walked to his grave to pay my respects.

What a view Mr. Maxwell enjoys from his hill, how poetic is his netherworld perspective, his view of crisp golf shots and indifferent ones. This ancient landscape, once an Oklahoma dairy farm, he interpreted and shaped into a golf course. Now my favorite golf course architect lies in a state of sardonic observation, as players flail against his creation, he holds the upper hand from his cliff, his rising ground of rock and earth he made famous by planting a golf green and tee atop. This hill from which he watches the struggle now entombs him. And so I paid respect to the man who has so often tormented and inspired me. I strolled along the ridge on a secluded pathway overgrown with vines and prairie grass, to the grave of Perry Maxwell and stood with my hat in my hands.

I built a golf course next to my house because I saw a vision through the dense wooded hills, perhaps a vision like that which inspired Mr. Maxwell to carve up a dairy farm in Ardmore. It's been in my blood ever since childhood as empty tuna cans scavenged from the trash bin, transformed into golf cup treasures, pressed into the family lawn cut low with a Lawnboy mower.

My Dad had given me a set of golf clubs cut down to size, and not content with the occasional golf game at the municipal course, I designed my own course in the briar and stone-laced lawn of our split level home. The cans provided a perfect golf cup cutting tool and liner once the hole was cut.

Golf course architecture sticks to my brain like gum on the underside of a school desk...out of sight but always there. My office wall bears a framed certificate on fancy paper suggesting that I'm a college graduate. I must confess, however, that it was ill-earned. I cheated. The results of every college test I took were enhanced by using cheat sheets...at least it felt that way to me. Much of my test-taking wasn't really process learning so much as learning by rote. I didn't use paper for my cheat sheet, but instead I used the many golf courses I'd played, along with their landmarks, as a tablet upon which to etch the answers to any test-worthy lists. This is how I earned an undergraduate and a masters degree. In a sense, I'm an academic fraud with a photographic golf course memory. I remember just about every golf hole I've played and can place intangible lists upon these concrete images, laying the elusive alongside the immutable.

My earliest golf course memory was of a small neighboring town, a winding fifteen mile drive east on U.S. Highway 60. My Dad loved to play and would bring me along with his friends. I'd stick a three-iron up through my arm and side with the grip extending vertically beyond my shoulder and I'd play along behind Dad's foursome, bashing the ball down the fairway, then chasing it. That was my first impression of golf architecture, a bud of inspiration for the course that winds behind my house today.

In 1963, the nine hole Nowata Country Club was visible in a sweeping panorama including a few prairie stunted trees, some short hills and a round pond. A shelter of weathered wood shingles supported by four posts stood next to the first tee. Green fees were purchased in the general store across Highway 60. Gnarled grumpy fence posts strung with two-point galvanized wire bordered the first three holes on the right, a counter clockwise challenge to a right-handed slicer.

The town of Nowata reminds me of the movie, *The Last Picture Show*, with Jeff Bridges and Cybill Shepherd. This town to which my Dad brought me because we didn't have a public course to play in Bartlesville then, *this* place was the beginning of my life-long affliction. In it's mild form a hobby, in it's fuller sense a virtuous obsession, blended with water and grass and trees and hills. Today, golf balls litter our twelve-acre homestead like orphaned Easter eggs. There is a bucket of balls sitting on the first tee with corporate logos, balls beaten into shapes resembling Marty Feldman's head, balls the color of lemon and lime and others simply weathered to a dusty tan, creased and sublime, telling stories of flight and places they've been.

In the country store in Nowata across the highway from the first tee they sold green fees, along with Bama pies and Moon pies vying for attention on the chrome rack near the counter, next to the sleeves of Spaulding Dot golf balls. The Dot golf ball was my favorite ball, my companion of choice. While others played with GI Joe or a water wiggle, I pounded golf balls from tuna can to tuna can until darkness chased me inside.

Designing tin can courses is the venue of my search for perfection. A quest for enlightenment in a round of golf, and if falling short of that high ideal, perhaps settling for a little self-awareness, an awareness of the euphoric peak of my athletic accomplishment and the valley of my failure. Connection with my athletic and competitive self but also with the parts of me still unnamed, the unsure, the noble, the impossible. What can I accomplish in measured advances of progress and retreat, exhilaration and despair? Is golf simply an illusion of progress, a good walk spoiled?

Bobby Jones once said, "Golf is a game of considerable passion, either of the explosive type, or that which burns inwardly and sears the soul." In either instance, I'm badly charred.

11

There's a Tornado in My Coffee

If it wasn't for the coffee, I'd have no identifiable personality whatsoever.
~David Letterman

My son wrote his thesis for Honors Meteorology on the topic "The Genesis of Tornadoes". The Revelation of Tornadoes might be easier to explain. Tornado prediction is a non-linear dart tossed into the misty morning fog. It's fraught with downdrafts of hope and gusts of unfounded certitude.

Yet we want to know. The weather man interrupts World Series because we want to know. We want to know what to wear, when to hide and what to cancel. My son says that we examine the storm by it's path in a forensic sense and the weather experts have made progress in the way of identifying the beginning of a tornado, but there is still much to learn. They look at the debris field - the result of the power - rather than the germination because it's easier to see the aftermath rather than the seed. But the holy grail is the beginning, the incubation of the tornado.

As I discussed this idea with my son, Brandon, the thought occurred that my vices are similar. I have no idea how they begin, but I know the swath of destruction they wreak, like ravenous locusts devouring a cornfield, stalks to stubble. Take coffee for instance. Please…I've had enough.

It began with a lousy cup from a college dorm vending machine. Foul swill infused with white gunpowder creamer and three packets of sparkling white sugar masked the stale, sour-earth undertones of low-grade brew. I lived that lie for years until encountering the dark, woody, eye-widening Greek coffee at Mastoris Diner in Bordentown, New Jersey. Now, I'm up to three cups of premium a day, and my disdain for inferior coffee is a point of shameless pride.

My brother, the physician, prefers the sappy-sweet gas station latte spewed from high volume low-expectation dispensers. I'm an intolerant coffee prima donna preferring the ability to name acidity, body, aroma, finish and flavor. What's the aroma, the aftertaste, the finish on the palate? Is it nutty, balanced, woody?

And so I stood along a cold and wet soccer field one Saturday, longing for a better cup, while watching my niece Anna compete and remarking to my sister Debbie, the teacher, and my brother Greg, the preacher, that I had a problem. Well, I didn't actually say that, I thought it, in the context of our triangular discussion about what makes a vice.

I said, "Coffee is my vice," in a wistful and blindly nostalgic way, the way I once looked at the Marlboro man smoking a cigarette and herding five hundred cattle all alone. Just a man in the wilderness, on a horse chasing cattle, and smoking tobacco against a setting sun. Surreal, powerful, romantic addiction, the kind that looks and smells and tastes and feels right, empowering my senses to creative outbursts of enlightenment.

I know. It's a lie. But it's a legal addiction. A Grande Americano with a half-inch of steamed soy and one packet of natural cane sugar enriches my veins with supernatural energy and fluid ambition. Coffee, with it's accompanied rush of caffeine, sharpens my focus, prevents lethargy and refreshes my brain, with minimal negative side effects.

Coffee isn't just a social lubricant or sensual rush - it promotes professional excellence also. My sister is taking a new position teaching mathematics this coming school year. What does coffee have to do with math? It's the key to all mathematical theorems. "A mathematician," Erdös liked to say, "is a machine for turning coffee into theorems."

But when does the tornado begin? Coffee drinking begins as a vice, then becomes habitual, as in the title of the Doobie Brothers album "What Were Once Vices are Now Habits". But then in a remarkable turn of rationalization, coffee drinking becomes virtuous, vice to habit to virtue.

So I search for scientific justification. Coffee stimulates greater creative power and promotes attentiveness. Coffee is filled with antioxidants. Coffee empowers rulers and peasants. And by ignoring the research about the negative effects of caffeine, I can focus on the spiritual justification, the virtuous reasoning of thinkers like C.S. Lewis. Here's what Mr. Lewis says about abstinence as a mark of spiritual pride. "One of the marks of a certain type of bad man is that he cannot give up a thing himself without wanting everyone else to give it up...An individual Christian may see fit to give up all sorts of things for special reasons–marriage, or meat, or beer, or the cinema; but the moment he starts saying the things are bad in themselves, or looking down his nose at other people who use them, he has taken the wrong turning." I side with Mr. Lewis, refusing to be an abstaining bore viewing the addicted from my righteous tower of temperance.

Great coffee is the mysterious elixir, the beginning of commerce and the companion of sunrise. For example, Balzac said that coffee set him to writing, "Coffee glides into one's stomach and sets all of one's mental processes in motion. One's ideas advance in column of route like battalions of the Grande Armée. Memories come up at the double, bearing the standards which will lead the troops into battle. The light cavalry deploys at the gallop. The artillery of logic thunders along with its supply wagons and shells. Brilliant notions join in the combat as sharpshooters. The characters don their costumes, the paper is covered with ink, the battle has started, and ends with an outpouring of black fluid like a real battlefield enveloped in swaths of black smoke from the expended gunpowder. Were it not for coffee one could not write, which is to say one could not live."

And I owe gratitude to Danish philosopher Søren Kierkegaard, who "had his own quite peculiar way of having coffee," according to his biographer, Joakim Garff. Kierkegaard "delightedly seized hold of the bag containing the sugar and poured sugar into the coffee cup until it was piled up above the rim. Next came the incredibly strong, black coffee, which slowly dissolved the white pyramid. Then he gulped the whole thing down in one go."

So just be careful not to trust coffee to fuel your creative ideas. It should only be a means of turning on the spigot, not a substitute for creative energy. Not to mention the obvious similarity to alcohol. Abusers of both claim inspiration, but as most folks know, coffee and strong drink only tend to make bores more boring.

I still don't know how tornadoes germinate, nor how I came to crave java, nor how words wondrously jump onto a blank page like splashed coffee on a white polo shirt. While I consider this, I think I'll have another cup. I can't resist a swirling mystery.

12

Mosquito Dancing in the Fire Hall

Dancers work and they work and they work, and they master their skills so far that improvisation just comes flowing out of them. Their natural expression of the best they can possibly be comes out of them because there is no boundary to hold them back... That's the mentality that I'm trying to create, recreate and hold on to forever.

~ *Pete Carroll - football coach*

My wife Karen spent most of her childhood in Tabernacle, New Jersey, a small town on the edge of the pine barrens between Philadelphia and Atlantic City. I visited my wife's home during our courtship, and I remember the drive from the Philly airport with Karen and her sister, Dawn, crossing the Ben Franklin Bridge, escorting me through my first impression of the Garden State. New Jersey seemed anything but a garden. My expectation of farms, tomatoes, and waving corn was displaced by neon bars and x-rated dives along Route 70 in Camden, a strip of real estate unlike any garden I had seen in Oklahoma.

We arrived at the Mason's home in their extra car, a rusty green Chevy Nova that seemed to be pointed chronically towards the ditch due to an alignment issue, along with a front passenger door permanently stuck shut. Exiting the car was the moment I met my mother-in-law to be. Ann greeted me and I leaned in for a handshake, perhaps a hug, that awkward moment of feigned intimacy and geniality. Surprisingly, Ann kissed me on the lips. I had no warning and coming from a staid Midwestern culture of smug restraint, my pupils dilated and I shrunk into a speechless stupor. I looked around the neighborhood and saw towering pine trees and flora and garden looking stuff. The strip joints were gone. Perhaps this was the Garden of Eden where inhibitions are ground into compost? I soon discovered the affectionate kiss to be the common handshake of the Garden State. I was praying the rule didn't apply to toll booth guys from South Philly as I pulled up to pay a toll. A Stallone inflection of, "How *you* doin'?" was plenty of intimacy for me with South Philly as I handed him a five dollar bill.

It was my first family clue, the sign of what lay ahead and how the culture of my upbringing would collide with Karen's culture of origination. Karen's family is a party waiting to happen. My roots are firmly planted in the Midwestern loam of virtue, grounded in religious rationalism and the social gospel that harkens back to the 19th century. It's sensibility is rooted in the Dust Bowl of the 1930's Oklahoma panhandle and the hills and hollows of Northeastern Oklahoma. It's mantra is a tight-lipped aversion to enjoyment, a cautious rationale, skewed closer to sin aversion than unabashed fulfillment of the senses, which isn't to be confused with true inner joy which has an unassuming quiescence. Lest you mistake my caution for shame, let me disabuse you of that notion. My prudish pragmatism is a mark of gentle pride. In fact, I embrace my social dysfunction.

On the other hand, I have learned to greet and kiss other women with platonic boredom and disinterest. I've also adapted to the notion of life as a dance, understanding that most social functions in Tabernacle such as dances, weddings, and graduation parties happened at the fire hall. Our wedding reception was at the Emergency Response Center, across the street from the fire hall, because Karen wanted something *different*, since her entire social life from 1st grade up was at the fire hall where her Dad was the volunteer captain. His captaincy was ironic, because Karen set the neighborhood on fire during her Dad's fire hall tenure.

This community hub hosted birthday dances, fund-raising dances, anniversary dances, Fourth of July dances, Groundhog Day dances and Bee Gees dances. Any excuse to dance to great songs like, "Give me that old-time rock-n-roll, that kind of music just soothes my soul..." and "C'mon let's do the *Twist* like we did last summer" and the *Mashed Potato*, *Wooly Bully*, and the *Locomotion*. Karen carries herself with physical grace, mostly because of her dancing at the fire hall.

My memories of dancing are simpler. I was a genie in a song and dance revue during the spring of 1978 at Harding University. Rather than Dancing with the Stars we were dancing with the two-left-feet-inhibited. I've recently begun to dance again. I spent a weekend at my alma mater wistfully reminiscing about my dancing ineptitude while attending Spring Sing. Harding is a bastion of lots of things, but dancing doesn't come to mind. In fact, during my days at Harding the euphemism "choreography" was used to express the main event of Spring Sing, a decided repudiation of dancing and vile gyrations, a real-life parody of the movie *Footloose*. Now, I watch Spring Sing and genuinely enjoy the music and choreography, but there is a large unwashed swath of alumni who dance like me and Elaine from *Seinfeld*. We dance the mosquito dance, an arrhythmic collection of cattle prod moves, to no recognizable beat replete with confused facial tics akin to one who has biting mosquitoes in their socks and underwear.

Karen and I were enjoying coffee at Midnight Oil near the Harding campus one Spring Sing Weekend, and we chatted with David Fowler and David Hall, also Harding Alumni. We spoke about our dysfunction, our aversion to dance. In the noisy din of coffee-house conversation, Mr. Hall told us that he was one of those mosquito dancers. However, what Mr. Fowler and I heard was, "I am a Speedo Dancer." And so we sipped our coffee and reflected on how people change when they leave conservative academia. David Hall is a Pastor in his home church and he enjoys dancing in a Speedo. We had a good laugh when we realized what Pastor Hall said. He is a mosquito dancer like me.

God bless the mosquito dancers of the world. All we want is a little rhythm and grace, and perhaps a community, like my wife had at the fire hall. Mosquito dancers eventually learn to waltz, but we start with tape on the floor at a place where the standards are low. A place where everyone knows your name and they play a get-up-and-dance song by Neil Diamond, and all we have to do is stagger about and hug someone and shout, "*Sweet Caroline!*" I feel my left foot jitterbugging and my right foot moonwalking, I hope it's not a mosquito.

One of my few dancing moments

13

Gushing Well Water

"It is no secret that the greatest treasures are found in the most remote, inaccessible and difficult places where we must pursue them with great energy and even greater risk. It's the same with our lives."

~ *Craig D. Lounsbrough*

I once asked an old college buddy who loves extreme sports, "Why do you feel compelled to tie off a rope and jump from a cliff?" His reply was, "Life is not worth living unless there is a measurable risk of dying."

A measurable risk of dying or at least inflicting serious flesh wounds was a day to day phenomenon in our college house. Randy and I lived in Rector House, a haven of collegiate camaraderie and mischief. It's gone now, demolished, but in the spring of 1981, it stood awaiting a date with the wrecking ball. Rector House was my home for two years at Harding University and I shared this dilapidated house with eight guys. We had a pet mushroom in the bathroom and a front sitting porch where we watched girls walk to Sunday church. Boldly, we entered the pedestrian stream, as beauty presented itself, like a Rose Bowl float filled with floral sweetness that we could join without pretension, entering the parade as voyeurs and jesters under the guise of church-going righteousness. It was dating sans chivalry, diluted and without commitment. Speed dating before speed dating was a thing. A walk and a sit down in church, a little sermon and song with a girl you didn't have to ask out and without the fear of rejection. She even walked you home afterwards.

A cafeteria now occupies the site of Rector House. I harbor no sentiment for it's demise, nor any remorse for aiding in it's destruction. When we discovered the plan to raze the sagging white clapboard house, we had a memorial ceremony for our old house. My buddy, Ralph, was training for intramural shot put and had a 16 lb. shot in his room. The hollow core mahogany doors were the red capes in the bullring to Ralph's raging bull. Tossing gas on the bonfire, I told Ralph he wasn't stout enough to toss the shot ball through a door. He snapped up the shot defiantly, crouched, and burst upward with furious energy, hurling it across the room. A crash of splintering wood split the air and a gaping hole worthy of a 105mm howitzer provided fodder for stories the remainder of the year, but the story wasn't finished yet. Ralph spied my golf clubs and challenged me, "Bet you can't hit a ball through the wall." The temptation was irresistible, so I drew my Tommy Armour 3 wood and tossed a Titleist down on the dining room carpet. Eyeing the wall that hid Alan Adam's bedroom on the other side, I turned and spun mightily into the ball, sending it cleanly through the sheetrock. Garnering a pretty good lie on the other side in Alan's bedroom, I played it out into Rick Carpenter's open chest of drawers. I'm fortunate the screaming ball missed hitting a stud or I might have imprinted "Titleist" on my forehead. We didn't think about things like that though, or if we did, we took a chance. Taking chances is something we do frequently when we are young.

The irony is that we become more cautious and subdued as we age, yet young folk are wilder, thrill seekers, more willing to risk, having much more to lose with life stories still being written. Logically, we should become more and more daring as we age because we have already lived full, well-rounded lives and should be ready to meet our Maker if we step back off a cliff ledge at ninety years old.

Many of my risk taking experiences happened while participating in extreme sports before extreme sports were invented as opportunity bred with vacuous collegiate boredom. Time and space gave birth to youthful stupidity and at places called Sugar Loaf, Red Bluff and Bluff Hole we incubated arthritic joint conditions and assured our place on the medical agenda of future orthopedic surgeons. My best friend Rick Carpenter's shoulder surgery later in life was precipitated by an event called "down hillbilly skiing".

One autumn day we donned multiple winter coats along with several pairs of jeans and stood atop Red Bluff peering down through the leaves to the creek bed below. We were fearless, stupid, and undaunted with the wind in our faces and a triple espresso jolt of adrenaline coursing through our veins. From the top of the bluff to the stream at the bottom is a 300 foot vertical descent. We took off down the hill running helter skelter and to not slow down, but instead retard our speed by bouncing off saplings and catching them with our arm or shoulder. So we flew down into the valley and Rick caught a sapling hard and fast that spun him around like a rag doll in a washer spin cycle.

Strikingly, risk-taking is exactly the image we see expressed to readers of a supposedly conservative and staid book, the Bible. God exhorts us to expend our resources, to take chances, to die poor as it were, and in the process, we will not die but live eternally rich.

"For everyone who has will be given more, and he will have an abundance." - Matthew 25:29

In her book, *The Writing Life*, Annie Dillard expresses the same idea about writing. "One of the few things I know about writing is this: spend it all, shoot it, play it, lose it, all, right away, every time. Do not hoard what seems good for a later place in the book… give it all, give it now. The impulse to save something good for a better place later is the signal to spend it now. Something more will arise for later, something better. These things fill from behind, from beneath, like well water. Similarly, the impulse to keep to yourself what you have learned is not only shameful, it is destructive. Anything you do not give freely and abundantly becomes lost to you. You open your safe and find ashes."

My youthful wild oats were impetuous, thoughtless, spurious. Now, I'm more thoughtful and cautious. Is it possible to recover a youthful spirit, to spend freely, knowing inspiration will once again rise, from behind, from below, like gushing well water? Wisdom such as this is wasted on the young who will wake up tomorrow and find themselves in a field of dry bones, wondering why they are saving their money, their time, their creations, their energy. But it's great advice for anyone preserving inspiration in wax figures, over in the corner of a cobwebbed museum separate from the rest of our lives where velvet rope is carefully draped, the place where our faith sits rocking and reminiscing about how good it was when we were young.

14

Sonic Hearing and the Wisdom of George Eliot

"Salt is good, but if it loses its salty taste, you cannot make it salty again. It is no good for the soil or for manure; it is thrown away. Let those with ears use them and listen."

~ Words of Jesus written by Luke

It was payday, and my son was on a mission to earn money to pay for his new Apple laptop computer. He had driven home from Oklahoma University to celebrate his Mom's 50th birthday and had called me the day before. "Dad, can I come home a day early and work to earn a little money?" While in my office, Brandon breezed past and I caught a glimpse of the sophomore Meteorology student. My bookkeeper remarked, "Who was that?" "My Son," I said. She replied, "Why is his hair sticking up?" "That's just the style now," I told her. He looked like Dennis the Menace after walking through the hurricane dryer at the car wash.

Unfortunately for my son, he wasn't wearing the latest technological wonder, as advertised on late night television. It's called Micro-Plus, a hearing device for those seeking the supernatural hearing of Batman. This magical gizmo will amplify sounds allowing you to eavesdrop on words spoken within a one hundred foot radius. You'll be able to "Hear things you've never heard before" and answer these profound questions: "Have you ever wished you had sonic hearing?" and "Would you like to never miss another sound?"

These are great questions and bring to mind George Eliot in her book *Middlemarch*: "That element of human tragedy which lies in the very fact of frequency, has not yet wrought itself into the coarse emotion of mankind; and perhaps our frames could hardly bear much of it. If we had a keen vision and feeling of all ordinary human life, it would be like hearing the grass grow and the squirrel's heart beat, and we should die of that roar which lies on the other side of silence."

Hmmm. $19.95 to hear the grass grow and the roar of a squirrel's heart seems like a great deal, but I'm going to defer to the wisdom of George Eliot and keep my $19.95. George Eliot is correct. Our attunement to the world around us and it's passions...anger, joy, happiness, envy, hate, lust, despair, love...is finite, often reserved for our family and friends. Each of us balance emotional saturation with our need for private peace, solitude, and emotional survival.

In the Gospel of Mark, chapter 4, Jesus says, "Whoever has ears to hear, let them hear." Perhaps George Eliot has opened my ears to a new way of understanding that admonition. Folks who hear with finely tuned ears, the adjacent broadcast that is human comedy and tragedy, do so aided by the unfathomable divine spark that transcends Darwin's evolution of the strongest. Looking out for our neighbors, sharing in their pain and hurt, attending funerals and hugging through the tears, loving the unlovable, giving a tip at a restaurant along with eye contact and meaningful words to those who serve us; these behaviors are unexplainable by theories of species perpetuation. Perhaps that's the reason religion and faith endures and governments fade.

We have a chocolate lab, Abby, whose whole world revolves around the turning of the back door knob, the tell-tale sound of her human friends joining her backyard world. If I stand at the back door she will see me standing there, and will tilt her head slightly with her head cocked and ears perked, waiting for the metallic noise of the door knob tumblers signaling interaction with the people she loves.

We don't really need those fancy hearing devices for $19.95. Most of us just need the courage to turn our head slightly to one side and listen for those people turning the door knob, opening doors into our offices, our churches, our neighborhoods, our worlds. It happens everyday, all the time.

I admire those who enjoin the battle of frequency in human tragedy…missionaries, pastors, nurses, counselors, police officers, teachers, doctors…all hear a disproportionate roar that would exceed the coarse human emotion most of us possess and their frames bear up more sturdily than those of us with feet of clay. God bless those good folk who hear the roar of the grass growing and the frantic beating hearts of many while most of us live blissfully quiet lives on the calmer side of the roar.

15

A Choir of Donkeys and Angels

Music expresses that which cannot be said and on which it is impossible to be silent.

~ *Victor Hugo*

I had a reputation as a youngster that enshrouded me like cigar smoke hovering over Churchill on a still summer evening. I sang pretty well. I sang because my church sang acapella and everyone sang. If you stole our hymnals we would sing, because we knew the words and music by heart.

We sang during chapel at Harding University for an entire semester sans songbooks when a guy I know but won't incriminate hid 3,000 hymnals in an obscure corner of a storage area in the Benson Auditorium. And the only reason the books were found was that the American Studies Program of the Business School booked President Gerald Ford to speak on campus in that same auditorium. So, several months after the books were entombed, they were resurrected through efforts of the Secret Service detachment of former President Ford as they did their standard facility search. It didn't stop the Christians at Harding University from singing in chapel in the days before Powerpoint. We sang from memory. We had no choice. If we didn't sing, the rocks and the pews would burst forth in song. And so we sang using only the song leaders pitch-pipe as a mechanical helper, although there were some who viewed that instrument with suspicion along with pianos.

That reputation for singing brought with it expectations, responsibilities, and pressure. Because of the reputation my church esteemed for singing simply and beautifully, those who knew us well, believed singing must be passed along to each congregant like holy elixir. This wasn't true. Our church sang with a common passion but with a diversity of talent, like the host surrounding Jesus in the manger. Donkeys bellowed, cows mooed, chickens squawked. But while the barnyard animals made a loud noise, many of our church sang like angels hovering over baby Jesus, beautiful, surreal. And most of us were painted with the same reputational brush, "Hey, those Church of Christ folks can sing."

My music teach knew this about me, this reputation for hanging out with the church of unadorned singing. I was loitering in the hall outside Mrs. McDonald's 7th grade music class at Central Junior High, waiting for my 4th hour class while 3rd hour was still in session. Suddenly the door opened and Mrs. McDonald pointed a crooked finger at me. She said, "Come in here, I want you to sing." I sheepishly shuffled into the room and stood beside her piano. Her music was open to an Irving Berlin song, *"Mary's a Grand Old Name"*, and she jauntily began playing as I sang for the 3rd hour students. I finished and walked back out into the hallway. I was shy but never felt uncomfortable during the impromptu exhibition, perhaps because singing is easier than talking to a beautiful cheerleader. My heart seemed bigger when I sang, my mind calmer, my feet no longer mired in clay.

There is something evocative in the way our souls mournfully waltz to music when we bury our dead and stand taller when we sing the Star Spangled Banner. Our souls burn to the beat of rebellion and the disharmony of revolution when we are stupidly young, our souls soar sublimely as we sing to our children. Music gives voice to the broken, courage to our warriors, and megaphones to our injustices. And all of this articulated in tones which softens the calloused and awakens the indifferent. Music strums and hums and changes us in keys that sound more reasonable and beautiful than words alone. Music is the stuff that comes out of us when we can't speak, notes shaped like the essence of our unspoken emotions.

Ray Charles speaks of music in the biological sense, that it was a body part, or perhaps an organ or one of his senses. "I was born with music inside me. Music was one of my parts. Like my ribs, my kidneys, my liver, my heart. Like my blood. It was a force already within me when I arrived on the scene. It was a necessity for me – like food or water."

I wonder if music ever goes away? Do songs from our lives hang in the air forever, the shaped notes hanging in the ether? I still hear *Sunrise, Sunset* from our wedding day, and my wife singing *Hush Little Baby Don't You Cry* to our mortally injured dog Cocoa just hours before we took her to the vet and said goodbye. I hear pastel smocked teens singing *Up With People* at the old Bartlesville Civic Center in the Sixties, and the screams of teenage girls on the Ed Sullivan show as The Beatles sang, *I Wanna Hold Your Hand*. Like hot air balloons hovering over our world, musical memory shapes and influences our thoughts, our legacy, our souls.

My earliest musical memory came from furniture. My parents RCA stereo console doubled as fine furniture and music savant. I cut my teeth and the living room rug on Al Hirt's *Fancy Pants* and Herb Alpert's *This Guy's in Love*, which led me to a love of big brass and Chicago's *Beginnings*.

I remember walking down the aisle between scarred metal chairs at Green Valley Bible Camp to the strains of voices singing *Just As I Am* before I was baptized in the camp swimming pool. I hear Paul McCartney and Wings, *Band on the Run* driving west on Highway 60, travelling to a junior high golf tournament in Ponca City. The next year in Norman at the state high school golf tournament, I played the worst round of my competitive career, 88, and trudged down the seventeenth fairway, head down, distraught. From the open window of an apartment near the fairway, the Beach Boys soothed my sagging competitive soul with the soaring *Help Me Rhonda*.

And I sang when my daughter Lauren was born, alone in my car on a pastoral New Jersey highway, driving home from the hospital on a December night, "You don't know what it's like to love somebody, the way I love you." I sang with the Bee Gees as I drove and thought about how happy I was to be a father, serendipitous happiness, like I had found a secret door to Heaven. So I sang, although the sentiment with which I sang wasn't what the Bee Gees sang about. I didn't care, that's how I felt, like nobody understood the joy of having a daughter like I did in that moment, so I sang like Pavarotti in the shower.

I have a good friend and old college roommate from Harding University who can't sing but does anyway. He drove a white 1970 Dodge Charger and called it The General. We sang Jimmy Buffett's, *Son of a Son of a Sailor*, while driving in The General and sang Marshall Tucker Band's, *Can't You See What That Woman is Doin' to Me*, on Friday nights in our living room when we had no female companionship.

And when we attended ball games, we sang only the last line of the Star Spangled Banner, ...'and the home of the (Atlanta) Brave.' It was funny that Ralph loved music. He didn't seem the type to love music, but I often thought of Ralph later in life when I sang to my kids before I put them to bed. I sang *An American Trilogy: Dixie, All My Trials and The Battle Hymn of the Republic,* a trio of songs arranged by Mickey Newbury which originated as American folk songs from the 19th century and popularized by Elvis in the seventies.

I thought of the stories Ralph told me about being young and hearing about the Confederacy from his Mom and listening to songs about the South before bed. I was from the Great Plains and thought all Americans were like me, and yet one of my best friends still spoke of the South, and he spoke of the War of Aggression Against the Southern States and he laughed when he said it but I knew the truth buried in the humor was complex and textured and layered with pain, heartache, pride and honor.

And of course I married a beautiful Yankee from New Jersey. And so I sang that Trilogy of songs to my kids and thought about how great our country was and is and how we are all different, yet the same, and how many have died for that ideal. And that Ralph and I are friends despite being cut from different bolts of geo-political-cultural cloth.

We are unique, we are the same, and I sense that every time I hear *An American Trilogy* and every time I see the Stars and Stripes waving in the breeze while singing our National Anthem, which Ralph and I now sing with a different understanding, with the correct ending, standing older, but taller, more proud and respectful, and grateful.

Grateful that many have died fighting for the principle of freedom and liberty and the United States of America. And grateful that floating out there somewhere in our memory ether is a jukebox of music carved from our voices, hovering around us like Winston Churchill's ubiquitous stogie smoke that magically never blows away.

16

Stealing Back Cool from Kerouac

Let your soul stand cool and composed before a million universes.
~ Walt Whitman

"We are coming to Norman and have four tickets to the football game." "Kewl" was my son's response to my text. He misspelled it on purpose because it's cool. A common colloquialism birthed in nonconformity, repurposed with spelling.

I've always loved "cool" because it expresses not one meaning but many, a cross-pollinated adjective moving fluidly in many cultures and languages. An Anglo can say "cool" in Chinese (kù 酷) and it means essentially the same as in English.

Cool exudes an attitude of calmness as a philosophy of restraint against the heat of living. It's variously described and birthed in the beat generation of Jack Kerouac and his On the Road milieu from the decade of the Fifties and the jazz music of Miles Davis, John Coltrane, and Dizzy Gillespie. It's British version takes on a restrained outward behavior, a nonchalant gentlemanly Teflon-coating in the mold of Sean Connery, unhurried stylish avant-garde demeanor, shaken, not stirred. And then there's the American Hollywood version, James Dean. But my favorite cool is rooted deeply in the trials and response of the African-American soul, an aloof calm rebellion in the face of oppressive authority that was revealed in blues and jazz, eventually working its way into the music of Elvis, Eric Clapton, and The Beatles.

Cool was appropriated from the disenfranchised, the downtrodden, the voiceless who somehow found a megaphone in music and pride in defiant non-violent rebellion. It's a coolness of spirit against a raging world. It's a heart guided by a thermostat rather than the thermometer of the capricious adopting the lists of 'what's hot this year' whimsy.

It's also simpler than that. "Cool" expresses everyday conversational approval or admiration. "Cool" is an adjective used by young girls and old men, by hipster doofuses and country club blue-bloods.

Our modern attempts to articulate our approval and admiration in non-establishment tones relies on a word that was once original and nuanced, but now universally exhausted with everyday usage, a word used to describe a tone of subdued icy calm without too much emotion and just the right touch of nonchalance, but with an absolute seal of approval.

Two thousand years ago, folks saw the world through the lens of the pater familia, and the dominant view of Fatherhood was of authority and domination as opposed to compassion and gentle nurture. Jesus spoke of the Father in a revolutionary way, as a five-year old daughter might speak to her Daddy at story time. Once while tucking in my daughter Jenna when she still thought me omniscient, she made a request after I gave her a quick story and a kiss, apparently thinking it not enough intimacy from her father and that I was simply going through the motions. "Daddy, would you lay down beside me for a minute before you go?" And so when Jesus spoke of the Father, it was simply unheard of for the maker of Heaven and Earth to be spoken of as having the time to be a Daddy, to find His lost ones and to not only find them and redeem their lostness with open arms, but to "lay down" beside His children.

The culture into which Jesus preached and lived was male dominated and men could divorce wives whimsically and indiscriminately and treat children as an afterthought. Into this world Jesus speaks words of liberation. He tells of searching for pennies in the cracks of a rustic kitchen floor and a shepherd frantically running through the fields searching for a lost sheep. And a Father who runs to welcome his son home from a binge of Bohemian wanderlust, which reminds me of a famously cool guy, Jack Kerouac, and his book *On the Road*. Kerouac's book is stream of consciousness genius, compelling because it speaks honestly of what Luke 15:13 reports in one short sentence. Kerouac wrote an entire book on a taped together continuous feed of typing paper so he wouldn't have to stop typing to change the paper in the typewriter, an entire stream of raging thought, a reflection of what the prodigal son may have been thinking in another place and time.

Luke 15:11 Jesus continued: "There was a man who had two sons. The younger one said to his father, 'Father, give me my share of the estate.' So he divided his property between them. "Not long after that, the younger son got together all he had, set off for a distant country and there squandered his wealth in wild living.

I'm not sure Jack Kerouac ever found what he was looking for. He died of complications from cirrhosis and internal bleeding at the age of 47. This stunning thought of self-awareness is from his book *On the Road*:

"I woke up as the sun was reddening; and that was the one distinct time in my life, the strangest moment of all, when I didn't know who I was – I was far away from home, haunted and tired with travel, in a cheap hotel room I'd never seen, hearing the hiss of steam outside, and the creak of the old wood of the hotel, and footsteps upstairs, and all the sad sounds, and I looked at the cracked high ceiling and really didn't know who I was for about fifteen strange seconds. I wasn't scared; I was just somebody else, some stranger, and my whole life was a haunted life, the life of a ghost."

Kerouac was the son who eventually came home to live and die in Lowell, Massachusetts, his birth town. He was often called the Father of the Beat Movement, a title he did not understand. Once someone called him a beatnik, one of the beat generation and he replied, "I'm not a beatnik, I'm Catholic." Many of his diary pages reflected a search for meaning, crucifixes and other symbols of faith. His longing to be saved, to come home, can even be seen in his prose. "My whole wretched life swam before my weary eyes, and I realized no matter what you do it's bound to be a waste of time in the end so you might as well go mad,...the only people for me are the mad ones, the ones who are mad to live, mad to talk, mad to be saved." — Jack Kerouac, On the Road

Jesus had the temerity to describe the Father not as a aloof distant judge, but rather as a runner, a party planner, a hugger, a giver of second chances. Cool happens when the hotness and madness and speed that often rules our world is calmed, slowed and tempered by the blessed assurance of naked trust in the world to come, a world that sometimes visits us on earth in moments of grace, the heavens touching the parched and overheated in comforting coolness.

Most of us have Kerouac moments, when we open our eyes, perhaps in some street gutter, or a moment of pain or weakness, moments we realize 'we are somebody else, some stranger...living the life of a ghost.'

Those moments either consume us in wallowing narcissism or provide moments of turning, moments that let us run into the arms of God. Eden is restored in small moments of hope as foreshadowing of a coming eternal age. It's the Way, it's mercy, it's grace. It's calm and cool in the face of the heat of things we think we desire. It's the recognition that the one thing we long for is coming. That's pretty cool.

17

A Note in Each Pocket

Failures, repeated failures, are finger posts on the road to achievement. One fails forward toward success.

~ *C. S. Lewis*

I've carried a sense of insignificance and high achievement all my life. I'm not good enough, yet look what I've done. It's what motivates me and what frightens me. It's the yin and yang connecting my deficiencies with my arrogance. The balancing force, the counterweight, the thing that keeps me from flying into the weightless space of narcissism.

My daughter Jenna texted me this message: "Hey Dad, Punt Pass and Kick is on the NFL halftime show!" I was one of those kids. I have six gold Punt Pass and Kick trophies somewhere in my attic. I care little about that now. It was the center of my universe, however, as a nine-year old. My picture in the paper, trophies, peer respect, congratulations from the adults at church and school. For a kid struggling to develop an identity and a little self-confidence, it was all I had. On the one hand, I was an insignificant kid, and on the other, a local hero.

Harold Ramis was an American actor, director, and writer specializing in comedy. He played Egon Spengler in *Ghostbusters* and Russell Ziskey in *Stripes*, along with writing and directing *Caddyshack*, *National Lampoon's Vacation*, and *Groundhog Day*. I once heard Mr. Ramis speaking about the interdependence of his self-doubt and his self-confidence.

His rabbi once told him, "You should start each day with a note in each pocket. One note says, 'The world was created just for me today' and the other note says, 'I'm a speck of dust in a meaningless universe.' And keep them both because neither is true and both are true. So in a way my career has been completely self-aggrandizing. I'm the most pumped up, grandiose person in the world, and I'm still the same humble schmuck I was when I started. I have no confidence, and yet there is this body of work that exists behind me that seems to say that I did do something. I feel like I'm starting today on a new career, looking for that next piece of work that's gonna be exciting, that's gonna mean something to me, and that I'm gonna enjoy and do with people that I can really love and respect."

Indeed, we frame our work with episodes of self-doubt and great achievement and they don't work in isolation, but rather in partnership. We are all artists of contradiction, specks in the universe, yet endowed with incredible creative power and imagination. We are artists drawing pictures, creating shades and shadow using obstacles that block the light. We are cooks in the kitchen blending fire and water, marking the fine line between incredible taste and inedible ash.

Mortal humans hiking on a journey this side of death, made more alive when we feel the note in the other pocket, the one that says we are no better than cheese in a freezer case with an expiration date, yet somehow, marvellous, glorious, and wondrously made.

Psalm 139:13 For you created my inmost being;
you knit me together in my mother's womb.
14 I praise you because I am fearfully and wonderfully made;
your works are wonderful,
I know that full well.

18

The Beauty of Creative Destruction

"My most important piece of advice to all you would-be writers: When you write, try to leave out all the parts readers skip." ~ Elmore Leonard's 10 Rules of Writing

"Put down everything that comes into your head and then you're a writer. But an author is one who can judge his own stuff's worth, without pity, and destroy most of it." Casual Chance, 1964 ~ Colette

I have two faces. My nice face smiles on cue and stops at neighborhood lemonade stands, tosses five dollar bills in the tip jar when the barista is not looking, and eats blackberry cobbler with ice cream. My ugly face sprinkles tip jars with inconvenient change, mocks McDonald's eaters, and gulps three dollar venti soy americanos while sniffing ginger in the produce section at Whole Foods.

Successful people share a common trait: They have brightly lit bathroom mirrors, unlike the hotel furnished "mirror that lies" which Jimmy Buffett once sang about. Successful folks value self-assessment while embracing one unlikely character trait, self-deprecation, often useful when looking into mirrors that speak the truth.

Self-assessment shares the same ruthless process with creating a beautiful work of art. The creative process identifies what isn't beautiful, or to be politically incorrect, removing the ugly so the beauty will shine. For example, Beethoven's 5th Symphony is gorgeous perfection, but hidden behind the music are reams of discarded music that we never see, notes that Beethoven tried that didn't quite work, leaving behind what we know as the 5th. According to Callum Hackett, creativity and great music, as well as striding into each day with our best face "does not require a virtuosity capable of instantaneous perfection, it needs a honed sensibility of imperfection so that you can work persistently at alternatives until that sense evaporates and what remains is worth an audience."

Perhaps this inversion – the idea of creating beauty replaced with the destruction of ugliness – is why so many admirable people are self-effacing. Which comes around to my original statement about two faces, and my wife's theory about the correlation of eyesight and aging. It's what keeps us romantically together, our inability to see clearly at close range, the flaws, wrinkles and blemishes, and time etching our faces like Tecumseh Sherman marching on Atlanta.

Despite her theory, she is testing her romantic attraction to me, spitting in the face of imperfection like a hobo eating expired cheddar cheese. She just received five pairs of reading glasses from Peepers.com and she looks amazing in these stylish rims. Alas, when she wears these attractive lenses I fear closeness, and the power of attraction wrestles the dread of magnification. So I'm staying at a safe distance, distrustful of honing too intimate a sense of imperfection...but honing our sense of imperfection is necessary.

In his book, *Story*, Robert McKee writes, "Genius consists not only of the power to create expressive scenes, but of the taste, judgement, and will to weed out and destroy banalities, conceits, false notes, and lies."

If we are writing the story of our lives with our faces, we sometimes find our own beauty by identifying our ugliness, removing the lying mirrors and having the courage to wear the good glasses, the ones that spare no detail, and weed out our false notes, revealing what was there all along, a lovely symphony of beauty.

Last night I enjoyed a dinner of roast beef stew with my parents and missionaries from Ecuador who have a son, James. James has some challenges in his life, his eyesight is not great, and he is challenged in other physical aspects as well. He is small in stature, he's seventeen years old but looks fourteen. James wanted to see my pitch and putt golf course behind our house before dinner. So we walked out to the first tee where I have a bin of clubs and a five gallon bucket of balls. He just wanted to look at the course, but I said "Let's play!" I pulled out a nine-iron and a ball and we walked to the first tee and as we did, James informed me that he was left-handed. The clubs are all right-handed, so I said, "We'll just knock it around some with this right-handed club." I helped him with his grip, he had a Hank Aaron grip, left hand down on the grip and right on top. We switched the hands and I told him to swing with his shoulders and dance with his feet. He made it to the first green with Wayne Gretzky slap shots and Paul Bunyan wood chops, leaving behind a gleeful trail of busted turf and fleeing grub worms. And he giggled without reason, at least to my sense of giggling normalcy. Once on the green he whacked a twenty-footer screaming across the putting surface and it hit the pin and went in and he leaped into the air like Nicklaus in 1975 at the Master's on the sixteenth green when he holed a 50 footer to take the lead.

I noticed he didn't struggle with any of this stuff I've been talking about: Being authentic, ugliness, mirrors that lie. He was just James. Later on, after shooting some hoops and kicking a soccer ball, we sat in my theater room which has six reclining chairs. I sit in the front right chair because the front middle and front left are broken, they don't recline. James looked at my reclined chair as he sat in the middle front chair and tried to recline his and I told him it was broken. He sat back. We were watching the Cardinals-Dodgers game and I wasn't too chatty, as the Cardinals were down 6-1. Then he looked at me and said, "Why don't you put these two broken ones on the back row and two good ones on the front row?"

Creative destruction removes our broken recliners, our joyless soul. I'd never considered switching my recliners. Maybe I'm too lazy, perhaps my mirror lies. Maybe I'll get some glasses like James, the ones that see the world as a blessing, something to giggle about, even when you are playing golf from the right side and you are left-handed. Then I can be destructive, creatively I mean, tear things up, put my broken front row chairs on the back row, and smile with sweet emotion, chiselling away the ugliness like Michelangelo discovering David, naked and proud inside a great block of granite.

19

Sixty Years on a Chalkboard

"What does the brain matter compared with the heart?"

~ *Virginia Woolf, Mrs. Dalloway*

"Love is not the absence of logic, but logic examined and recalculated, heated and curved to fit inside the contours of the heart"

~ *Tammara Webber, Easy*

We celebrated our parents sixtieth wedding anniversary the day after Thanksgiving. While taking family pictures in the church sanctuary at the Dewey Church, I saw light emanating from the holy of holies, the door leading to the inner room where some of my family had changed into baptismal garments before being immersed in living water. As children, we were not allowed to venture into this mysterious hallway.

My brothers and I walked to the open door and peered inside to see what mischief our college and high school age sons were finding in the mysterious hallway leading to the baptistery.

Stashed in this hallway near the podium on the north side is a large chalkboard on wheels. We watched as Brandon, Jacob, and Drew expounded on the world they know, wielding only a stick of chalk and their minds and a language that they understand, meteorology, math, and physics. The chalkboard was covered with equations that I didn't understand, pulse compression, calculus, algebra, for all I know they were working toward an understanding of silly string theory. I understood none of it and realized this generation is closing in fast and I lack their savvy and skills.

We Taylor brothers are not mathematicians. I'm a homebuilder, Toby is a physician, and Greg is a Gospel minister. All three of us married women of numbers, high school math teachers. Our sons received from their mothers the gift of numbers, data, quantity, structure, space, models, and change. Many of our daughters and nieces embrace the gift of poetry. The rhythm and grace of a healthy considered meal deliciously cooked by my daughter, Jenna, the dietetics major. The expressions and elegance and passion of Toby's daughter Emma singing a lovely Broadway song called "Pulled" from the Addams Family musical during our family talent show. And my niece, Hannah, expresses her poetic gift as a wonderful writer, nurse, and friend to seemingly everyone she touches.

We are poets and mathematicians. When children are born, we write poetry and explore possibilities. When we celebrate sixty years of marriage, we marvel and do the math, comparing our own marriages by fractal comparison, our own married tenure compared to the celebrated one. Possibility and reality, beginning and end, poetry and mathematics, the story lived out in the days between those bookends.

I remember vacationing in Orlando with my family as a sixteen year old kid. I flew back alone to Tulsa for a golf tournament. I remember that first jet trip as a coming of age moment, even as I felt alone leaving my family in Orlando. I felt a sense of independence that my Dad and Mom had enough confidence in me to let me fly back alone. I flew Delta Airlines and listened to canned airline music on my headphones from the early Seventies and late Sixties, Eric Clapton's *"Layla"* and *"Marry Me Bill"* by the Fifth Dimension. It wasn't quite as manly a coming of age moment as the Inuit Indians sending off a sixteen year old brave into the Arctic Sea in a sealskin canoe to hunt for caribou on a distant island, but it made me feel grown up. I also listened to Carly Simon sing *"Well That's the Way We've Always Heard it Should Be"*, singing about her parents and about how she thought marriage was supposed to be and how it really was...

"I tiptoe past the master bedroom where, My mother reads her magazines. I hear her call sweet dreams, But I forgot how to dream. But you say it's time we moved in together, And raised a family of our own, Well, that's the way I've always heard it should be: You want to marry me, we'll marry."

I remember the hauntingly beautiful voice of Carly Simon singing about parents who had failed to convey and live out the dream, marrying for no reason other than it's the way I've always heard it should be.

Mom and Dad gave us no sense that love and marriage was easy. We saw the tears, the hurt, the trials, not just of marriage but of life. The poetry, the math, the story written with chalk on a sixty-year-old board, scrawled with equations spilling over the borders, overflowing with love and imperfection, grace and blessings, family and friends.

Thanks for teaching us poetry, Mom, and thanks for doing the hard math, Dad, and for writing a story that never really ends. It lives on in holy places, back alleys, and in mysterious hallways on blackboards filled with equations, poetry, and stories that overflow the margins of our understanding.

20

Walking to Heaven in Twenty Mile Moments

Faithless is he that says farewell when the road darkens.
~ *J. R. R. Tolkien*

I stood in the tiny foyer of the holy of holies recently, the old knotty pine auditorium of the Tabernacle church of Christ, remembering my wedding day, June 15, 1985. Thom Mason fidgeting and pacing, preparing to walk down the aisle and give away his daughter, Karen, to the likes of me. In the front corner of that auditorium, surrounded by the mops and brooms of a janitor closet the size of a phone booth, I received a marital blessing before Roger Hladky performed the official rites. Rick Carpenter, my best man, my brothers Toby and Greg, and Ralph Rowand, prayed that I would not faint and that our marriage would be blessed. Twenty-nine years later I still pray near brooms and mops and call those five men some of my best friends, and that twenty-two year old beauty is still my love, my wife.

Last week, my Oklahoma friends asked where I was headed for the weekend and I told them New Jersey, to the shore, the "Wawa", and the Tabernacle. They understand the shore. I tell them "Wawa" is an Ojibwe Indian word for coffee at sunrise and hoagie at sunset, and they understand that also. But the Tabernacle takes some breath to explain.

Acts 1:8 says you will be my witnesses in Jerusalem, Judea, Samaria and from Nottingham, England to Philadelphia, from New Jersey to California. William Cutts was a pebble splashing into a spiritual pond, a witness for Christ who settled with his father in Tabernacle, New Jersey, after coming over from Nottingham, England in the middle of the nineteenth century. William walked twenty miles round trip from his farm near Tabernacle on many a Sunday, to catch a train in Medford and on to Philadelphia, to the nearest church he could find that resembled the one from his youth in Nottingham, England, a church born of the English restoration. William's funeral in 1914 was the catalyst for the beginning of the Tabernacle church, a funeral preached by E.E. Joynes who would become the preacher at the Tabernacle church from inception in 1914 until 1947. Because of William's witness, the church has grown and spread across communities, states, and nations.

Sometimes we see heaven on earth. If heaven can be compared to unquenchable oceans in massive unseen underground reservoirs where God's will and work is always done, occasionally the unseen becomes seen in springs of living water and the veil is pulled away and heaven nourishes earth in previews of transcendent beauty and love. This past weekend I tasted the water from that unquenchable well.

I'm a gentile from Oklahoma, an adopted son, but a common believer at Tabernacle, born into this church faster than I could eat baked goods from Rhonda Kate Cutt's kitchen and sing a verse of "A Common Love". It's a church like my own family. As Robert Frost once described it, "a place where, when you go there, they have to take you in."

With a God-honoring compass and scriptural map, the Tabernacle Church is a gathering place where memory is honored and hope is fostered and love is practiced, where strangers in a strange land gather to nurture and reveal the fountain of living water that springs from reservoirs that never go dry. This church has been an oasis, a cup of cold water at Jacob's well, where God is worshipped with passion and sinners are taken in with tenacious love.

Today, many choose spiritual shortcuts, forgoing the long road of perseverance. Sound bite twitter posts and flying thumbs have replaced callused hands. One hundred years ago Christians gathered in Tabernacle to worship with songs echoing in the pines as they became Jesus hands.

John Donne wrote, "Reason is our Soul's left hand, Faith her right, by these we reach divinity." Sometimes we seek salvation in nanoseconds of emotion and we forget the long walk and how callused hands and blistered feet are the way to reach the Divine.

So I stood in that foyer staring at the pine-clad walls of the inner sanctum, the place where our marriage began in 1985. Karen walked up to me and we strolled down the aisle once again, backwards, as if by some act of ritual we could reverse the years, be kinder, love more, pray more, worry less, give away more. And be more grateful for those who walked before us, sometimes twenty miles on a Sunday, to the City of Brotherly Love.

George Eliot once wrote, "The growing good of the world is partly dependent on unhistoric acts; and the number who lived faithfully a hidden life, and rest in unvisited tombs." This weekend as the Tabernacle church celebrated 100 years of faithful life and worship, I walked backwards through time with my bride, paying respects to those who have walked before us without fanfare, just doing the work of Jesus in this corner of the world, those who have lived faithfully a hidden life, and rest in unvisited tombs, at least unvisited by the modern world, although I somehow sense their spirit is visited daily by people who in their own time and place walk with faith. They've chosen the long and narrow path, the difficult and often rejected way.

If you look carefully, God gives us a snapshot of those moments to come, where the world is restored to its rightful design, where everywhere you look you find beauty and perfect relationship, where hugs replace darkness, smiles erase anger, a place where love flows like eternal springs.

I went to Tabernacle, what my bible calls "a dwelling place", where once upon a time God's presence travelled in a tent. Someday, God will make His home among men and women once again and there will be no tears. That twenty-mile walk will be much easier, just a stroll across the room, in a place where all is beautiful, relationship is restored, and the singing will surpass any beautiful noise you've heard before. It will be a lot like this weekend where the Okies sat next to Californians as dust bowl stoics danced with the high-handed, and Texans nodded joyfully swaying shoulder to shoulder with Tennessee Volunteers, and the can't-contain-their-joy-bobble-headed singers swelled to the Hallelujah Chorus, an ocean of souls that would not be quiet, God's choir singing and swaying in perfect harmony in the Tabernacle of God.

Sometimes Heaven and Earth overlap, and sparks fly and angels sing and the world appears complete and perfect. I never made it down to the shore, didn't set foot in a Wawa, but I did see God's reign come down to earth, a coming attractions glimpse of where William Cutts was walking twenty miles on a Sunday. Think I'll lace up my shoes and take a walk.

21

It's Sweet to Play Like You are Loved

"In golf, you don't beat the other golfers—you beat your self-doubt. That's why I don't play, because I can't beat anyone—not even myself."

~ Jarod Kintz

One of the most memorable rounds of golf I've ever played came on the heels of an exchange with a man we called Sweet, even though decorum and his given name, Edward Muir Sweet, demanded we call him Mr. Sweet. The elimination of the honorific "Mr." was not an insult. The one syllable surname "Sweet" simply rolled easily off our tongues as an endearment that bridged the years separating us. He didn't demand the formality, nor did he demand we call him by the name most used to greet him, "Tid". He gave us license, and so, to us, he was "Sweet", a friend, from a generation we sometimes suspected. It was after all the age of Watergate.

The exchange happened between the morning and afternoon rounds of the Russell Lipe tournament, hosted by Sooner High School and College High School. The year was 1977 and I had just walked off the 18th green hotter than Bobby Knight in a chairless room at a referee convention. I've often wondered about the role emotions in the games we play, how emotions sometimes elevate us and other times make us lose our minds and our games.

After storming off the 18th green, I walked into the pro shop at Adams Golf Club and approached the counter as Sweet watched me walking towards his position of command and control. Sweet had a salt and pepper military flat top and horn rim glasses, along with a graceful bearing and natural rapport with the kids who played golf in his domain as golf shop manager. However, I was angry and wasn't looking to chat. I said to Sweet, "Give me a sleeve of Titleist, a ham and cheese, and a Coke." Sweet asked me, "How did you play this morning? You doing ok?"

He was always the gentleman, although any abuse we heaped on him was returned two-fold. Sweet took time for putting contests with junior golfers and the putting clock challenge was often a masquerade for a counselling session and the conversations that often occurred between an older, wiser man, and a youngster full of bravado masking post-pubescent insecurity. We were challenged to not only beat Sweet in a putting contest, but to match wits with someone who had seen a lot more of the world than we had, a transfusion of life from the wise to the rose-cheeked innocent in the midst of rolling golf balls on a broad expanse of tightly mown green grass. Sweet wanted to know how I was doing, and I replied with one word, "79".

Golf is a game that reveals you and your score always speaks the truth. We often repeated this cliché', "They don't ask how, just how many." Style matters, but in the end, only the score rings true. Golfers wrestle the demons of self-expectation often reverting to their own statistical mean. Our self-expectation is a subliminal weakness when we are well, a visible strength when we are playing poorly. We are weakest when playing well although often blind to our softness. Our strongest moments often come in the midst of our poor play. Like the Bible says, we find strength in our weakness. Sometimes that strength manifests itself in outward emotion, even anger.

I remember the first time I heard the term, "I can't stand prosperity." It was playing with a buddy and he was four under par and had just hooked his second shot on a par five into the creek. No cursing, no club throwing, just "I can't stand prosperity." Exceeding our own competitive expectations seems to be self-correcting, almost spiritual, beyond our control, determined by the gods of golf. It's a self-regulated mechanism, returning you to a zone of comfort not unlike a thermostat that senses when you've gone too hot or too cold.

Great golfers, indeed great athletes, have shoved the needle of expectation higher than anyone else. In golf, the nomenclature is "go deep" or "go low" or "unconscious." But once you begin to go low, how do you keep your foot on the pedal? Who has the competitive nerve, the brass tenacity to go lower. A 62 somehow makes one a golfing genius. But there is baggage. There are dues to pay and few can pay them. Many have the physical talent to play great golf, but to maintain a level of excellence throughout a four-hour round of golf, that's brave, that's crossing into the realm of faith and belief that you are better than those around you. Maybe even better than…yourself?

Prosperity is difficult to bear and, yes, it does demand a huge dose of athletic arrogance and superiority. It's not something one can pretend. It has to bear some semblance of reality grounded in performance, grounded in the weight of expectation in not only your own mind but in the mind of your competitors.

It's like accepting grace with gusto, without apology. Understanding that you are the one most deserving and worthy of excellence, as if by birthright. But is anger indicative of this birthright?

As I walked out of the golf shop that April day after firing a lousy 79, I told Sweet, "I'm shooting a 66 this afternoon." Sweet looked at me like I was a stupid kid who should just keep his mouth shut and play. But as I walked out the door, angry and determined, I muttered, "Just watch, you'll see," and I pushed open the glass door, cleats clacking on the asphalt path to the first tee.

I parred the first hole, a short par four. My coach, Ken Bruno, was playing the adjacent eighth hole and as I walked off the second tee box towards my tee ball, bag lashed against my back, eyes scanning the ground a step ahead, Coach said something to me. He rarely spoke to me while I was playing, but this time he did. "Keep your dauber up," he yelled over at me, noticing my head down. Maybe he had heard about my 79. I had no idea what a dauber was but it annoyed me. I already had my mind set on what was going to happen and I thought his well-intentioned admonition might take the edge off my anger. I didn't want to keep my dauber up. I wanted to punch someone in the dauber.

I birdied hole two. I came to the eighteenth tee five under par. All I needed was to carry the creek 220 yards out, in the fairway, then a sand wedge and a putt for 66. I missed a twenty footer and settled for par and a 67. I won the tournament. Did my expectational barometer simply self-correct? Why does anger cause some athletes to focus and others to lose their minds?

Bob Knight, the legendary Army, Indiana and Texas Tech basketball coach writes in his book, *The Power of Negative Thinking*, "...recognizing, addressing, and removing obstacles to winning, is the formula for success on the basketball court and in life." For Mr. Knight, that includes preparation and elimination of mistakes. Victory, he writes, "favors the team making the fewest mistakes." Coach Knight won three NCAA basketball championships so it's difficult to quibble with his coaching style, a mix of berating players like a drill sergeant, throwing chairs, and identifying weaknesses for the purpose of correction.

Scott Nagy, the head basketball coach for the South Dakota State Jackrabbits uses another coaching paradigm with this slogan, "Play like you are loved." According to The New York Times, quoting Nagy, during the 2013 NCAA basketball tournament, "We don't run around like we're in a lovey-dovey commune, but what I want our guys to know is that family, teammates, and coaches love them and that you don't have to perform in order to know that you are loved." Coach Nagy's team speech before the conference championship game ended with this: "I want you to play like you're loved. Play freely. Love isn't dependent on your performance. No matter how you play, you are loved. Play with that in mind." That's not exactly the same as a coach who insults your manhood by telling you your jockstrap is pink because you won't step up and take a charge.

Play like you are loved. Play angry. Play by removing the negatives. All three can be valid, but one aspect shared by each is this: Play freely. Each competitive style calls for the freedom to play without inhibition. Freedom from self-loathing and freedom from conscious analysis. In a sense we get out of our own way and let our subconscious rule our play. There are no limits, there are no obstacles, there is no doubt about our worthiness to not only "stand prosperity" but to revel in our good performance and to let it all hang out.

I'm still trying to figure out how to play optimally. Perhaps great golf is more than a 67. It's playing as a gentleman, granting and accepting a gracious spirit of friendship, cultivating integrity in the midst of competition, along with being a good companion in the midst of a four-hour walk. At fifty-three years of age, I've given up on playing angry. No longer do I slam wedges into the ground, snapping the shaft in white-hot anger at a missed shot. As for the power of negative thinking, life's too short to think about removing all my obstacles. So I'm choosing to play like I'm loved. It seems to make more sense to me now. Indeed, it's Sweet to play like you are loved. I'm grateful to Mr. Edward Muir (Tid) Sweet who taught me many years ago about the spirit of competition along with how to play like you are loved...even if I didn't realize it at the time.

22

Saying Goodbye to Jimmy

"Friendship is the hardest thing in the world to explain. It's not something you learn in school. But if you haven't learned the meaning of friendship, you really haven't learned anything."

~ *Muhammad Ali*

Butch Cassidy and the Sundance Kid was a great movie not because those two were charming thieves, but because it's a love story. What better way to die than to go out with your best friend, fill both hands with six-shooters, and charge into the sunset screaming toward a hailstorm of bullets? At it's essence, a love story, not Robert Redford and Katherine Ross, but rather, Redford and Paul Newman.

Maybe that's what is so great about watching that movie. Guys really struggle to keep lifelong friends, and these two guys, even though they robbed trains and burros carrying currency, stayed together the entire journey. Girls are naturals at friendship; Guys, not so much. Reminds me of something Stephen King once wrote, "Friends come and go in our lives like busboys in a restaurant." Sometimes, they simply go home.

My cell phone rang on a Sunday in May and I knew it was Jimmy. I said goodbye to Jimmy although I had no surety of goodbye, only the palpable sense of completion that comes with finishing a great book, that our friendship was graduating summa cum laude, and that we had both been blessed by our friendship beyond understanding.

Jimmy had just been released from OU Medical Center. He had been given bad news and his brother David had given me the details. I walked into my back yard and sat next to the pool, remembering another pool where I was baptized, at Green Valley Bible Camp on a sweltering July day.

Jimmy and I talked like the old friends we are. We haven't stayed in touch much through the years, but we melt back into conversation like warm butter on hot corn. We talked about his Dad, William, who is buried beneath a headstone that reads, "A great man has fallen" II Sam - a reference to 2nd Samuel in the Bible - which was sounded out by his brother-in-law as "A great man has fallen, aye-aye sam." In the face of grim news Jimmy still laughed like he did in the old days, when we were young and smart and knew things. His voice was peaceful, calm, measured, intelligent, even as our conversation was tinted with brokenness, our voices cracking with emotion, laughing and crying all at once.

He was my coming of age friend, the friend Richard Dreyfuss, playing a writer reminiscing about his youth recalled, as he typed on a crisp white page in the final scene of the movie, *Stand by Me*, "I never had any friends later on like the ones I had when I was twelve." The good friends never fade away. They live on, they inhabit our souls and our hearts as they touch us from a distance with the music we made together and when I hear that music, Jimmy's full-throated laugh and dancing brown eyes light the hallways of my memory.

I feel Jimmy at my side when the church sings *Just As I Am* and it's 1972 at Green Valley Bible Camp as Jim and I stand together singing,

"Just as I am, thy love unknown hath broken every barrier down".

I hear Jim's easy laughter as I tell stories, my first recollection that storytelling inhabits my soul, riding on a bus to that same church camp, two of my buddies, Jim and Tim, sat listening as I told a story fabricated from details I saw through the bus window. I was born a storyteller on that bus and I was born again in that camp pool a few days later, a story begun and a second birth, writ from places once dark with Jimmy by my side, helping to light a lamp in dark places with that laugh and gentle humor.

That summer we listened to The Eagles *"Take it Easy"* and Bill Withers *"Lean on Me"* on Jimmy's low tech cassette recorder. It was my first memory of my own music, or at least my own through my friend Jimmy.

"Sometimes in our lives , we all have pain, we all have sorrow, but if we are wise, we know that there's always tomorrow..."

~ Bill Withers

Jimmy was a wonderful pianist and one of his favorite artists was Billy Joel. We hung out in his room listening to Joel's *"The Stranger"* and the album *Toulouse Street* by The Doobie Brothers. Jimmy and I managed to float the Illinois River just about every year from 7th grade through my senior year in high school. We once lost a canoe under a fallen tree in the fierce outer current of the river. We jumped from the trusses of the river bridge and lived. We talked about God. And when we paddled past a couple of girls in a canoe, our senses heightened and we grew silent, waiting for conversational privacy to evaluate what we had just seen, and plan accordingly, perhaps to casually bump into them later downstream, maybe tip their canoe... What did we know? We just knew girls made us goofy.

We were two kids learning how to live without a filter, without someone peering over our shoulder, here on our swirling river as beauty and hormones competed for our attention along with God's great outdoors and our innate mischief.

Jimmy was fifty-four when he passed from this life on July 14th, surrounded by his family.

He told his older brother Eddie, "I'm going to see Pop first." He said goodbye in the same graceful and light-hearted way that he lived, revelling in his answers to aggressive sales folks on the phone when asked why he was cancelling his phone service or subscriptions, "The reason I'm cancelling is I'm dying, I'm going home."

I miss my friend, although I still hear his tenor voice when the church sings *Just As I Am*. I still see his shining eyes when *Lean on Me* comes on the radio. I still see the back of his head every time I sit in a canoe, and whenever I hear the Eagles, I think of Jimmy and think I never had any friends later on like the ones I had when I was twelve. Jimmy lived with a faith that moved mountains and someday I'll see him again, I believe that, and look forward to one day sitting on a crystal clear river floating in a canoe looking at the back of Jimmy's head, wondering how he'll be different, how he'll be new, and how amazing the music will sound dancing off the sparkling surface of a perfect flowing river.

Until we sing again, Dr. Jim Burns, my good friend, may the Lord bless you and keep you, and make His face shine upon you, and give you peace.

Dr. James Burns

23

Why My Son doesn't Look like Cary Grant

I had no idea of the character. But the moment I was dressed, the clothes and the make-up made me feel the person he was. I began to know him, and by the time I walked onto the stage he was fully born.

~ Charlie Chaplin

One of my best friends has a son who works at J.Crew. My son has a summer job driving the trash truck to the dump and he shops at Goodwill. But I think I've figured it out. It's genetic, the why I mean. The *why* of why I dressed like an idiot until buying a few suits and working as a CPA at the age of twenty-eight. Before then I was like Steven Wright in his story of meeting a beautiful girl, "I met this wonderful girl at Macy's. She was buying clothes and I was putting Slinkies on the escalator."

Escalators are more interesting than buying clothes at Macy's, but my youthful rebellion pales compared to that of my son. His youthful defiance by expressions of sartorial deconstruction bypasses Slinkies and detours to the local thrift store buying freshly out of style duds at the price of dirt.

Here's what John Waters, the director of the 1988 movie Hairspray, says about fashion tips for men. (It's as if Mr. Waters crawled into my son's closet, took a quick picture of the dissonant display of cotton, wool, and leather and then wrote this paragraph.)

"You don't need fashion designers when you are young. Have faith in your own bad taste. Buy the cheapest thing in your local thrift shop — the clothes that are freshly out of style with even the hippest people a few years older than you. Get on the fashion nerves of your peers, not your parents — that is the key to fashion leadership. Ill-fitting is always stylish. But be more creative — wear your clothes inside out, backward, upside down. Throw bleach in a load of colored laundry. Follow the exact opposite of the dry cleaning instructions inside the clothes that cost the most in your thrift shop. Don't wear jewelry — stick Band-Aids on your wrists or make a necklace out of them. Wear Scotch tape on the side of your face like a bad face-lift attempt. Mismatch your shoes...go to the thrift store the day after Halloween, when the children's trick-or-treat costumes are on sale, buy one, and wear it as your uniform of defiance."

Mr. Waters was sitting on Brandon's left shoulder in every Goodwill store he entered screaming into his ear, "Ill-fitting is always stylish!" And I was on the right shoulder, whispering clichés about tucking in shirts as we pushed open the glass doors of Kohl's and breathed deeply the fragrance of mass retail. I whispered, "Hey, Brandon, how about this pair of Bass Weejun Loafers in basic black? You can keep spare change on top of your shoes!", while the devil Waters replied, "Go ahead, look like your Father, I won't say a word, the penny loafers will scream it out like a hobo eating baloney courtside at a Lakers game."

Young men eventually want to look like their Father, when they were flat bellied, sleek and dressed like Archibald Alexander Leach before he changed his name to Cary Grant and became the stylish movie star icon of a generation. Guys search for distinction by embracing the offbeat. They want it both ways. They don't want to be like anybody, but they want to be like somebody. They want to look like Cary Grant and still be Archibald Alexander Leach. Ah the horror... how to fit in yet stand apart in expressive sartorial splendour.

My Son, Brandon

So how do you embrace style but not conformity? In the words of Jean-Claude, the French pea of Veggie Tales fame in the castle scene (stolen from Monty Python) while expressing incredulity at their ability to clap hands when they had none (they were peas after all), "I have no idea."

Cary Grant, however, does have an idea. The actor wrote an article for *This Week* magazine in 1967, discussing the finer points of men's fashion. Here are a few of Mr. Grant's tips:

- "I've purchased dozens of suits over the years and they all have one attribute in common: they are in the middle of fashion... In other words, the lapels are neither too wide nor too narrow, the trousers neither too tight nor too loose, the coats neither too short nor too long."

- "It's better to buy one good pair of shoes than four cheap ones... The same applies to suits, so permit me to suggest you buy the best you can afford even though it means buying less."

- "Do see that your socks stay up. Nothing can spoil an otherwise well-groomed effect like sagging socks."

- "Don't be a snob about the way you dress. Snobbery is only a point in time. Be tolerant and helpful to the other fellow — he is yourself yesterday."

- "Wear, not only your clothes, but yourself, well, with confidence. Confidence, too, is in the middle of the road, being neither aggressiveness nor timidity. Pride of new knowledge — including knowledge of clothes — continually adds to self-confidence."

I'm becoming Cary Grant. Naaah, I don't look like that, but I do agree with Mr. Grant's clothing sensibility. And I no longer give apparel advice to young men. They can figure it out in their own good time. Somehow, I've come home to roost in the middle ground between the dull pragmatic racks of Kohl's and the slick blur of stylistic nuance at J. Crew. It's comfortable here, in the middle ground between Archibald Alexander Leach and Cary Grant, resting in the sartorial nest of common sense and English decency.

24

Yesterday I Saw You Smile

Yesterday you awoke
in the Africa room at Nam's
crying in the dark
and I stumbled to your crib
sleep-starved
I picked you up and took you
to the day bed where you nestled
into the crook of my arm
and we slept until dawn
without moving

Yesterday we drove to church
and you were lulled to sleep
by the ribbon of highway
I carried you into the sanctuary
your matted damp hair
and baby breath warming my neck

Yesterday you ran into the parking lot
and you fell
your head against the asphalt
made the sound of a thumped melon
and a baseball grew from your forehead
You screamed...I screamed, silently
not wanting to alarm you
and I held you

Yesterday you were a whirling dervish
a soccer prodigy run amok
running circles on the field
boundless energy
Mr. Charlie, your game referee
told you to "keep smiling, keep having fun,
you have a great gift, treasure it
someday you will do that in college."
I knew it was true
as I grabbed your hand and we walked to the car

Yesterday I stood at the top of the bleachers
at Union Stadium
and I yelled "She's out"
as you lined up a free kick from forty
You made a powerful strike
and the ball screamed upward
to the goal
over arms of the keeper
who knew immediately, but too late
she began backing up, backing up
but not enough, over her finger tips
the ball passed just under the bar
like a happy dream
Goal!
"That was impressive"
I heard Leslie say, and I thought,
"Yes, yes it was."

Yesterday
you wore jersey 11
and the arm band of captain
You took charge
chasing the ball full tilt
diving, lunging, whatever it took,
Our spirits soared with you
as you lay on the grass
and the clock said 1:11
I thought of the prophet Charlie
I hugged you
through the grit and grass
the debris of victory

A captain run amok
the field tilting to your joy
the thrill of being one with
the pitch, the ball, the goal…yesterday

Yesterday I saw you smile   (To Jenna from Dad, November 2012)

25

Skimming Along Old Man River

I remember that as I was writing a poem on "Snow" when I was eight. I said aloud, "I wish I could have the ability to write down the feelings I have now while I'm still little, because when I grow up I will know how to write, but I will have forgotten what being little feels like." And so it is that childlike sensitivity to new experiences and sensations seems to diminish in an inverse proportion to growth of technical ability. As we become polished, so do we become hardened and guilty of accepting eating, sleeping, seeing, and hearing too easily and lazily, without question. We become blunt and callous and blissfully passive as each day adds another drop to the stagnant well of our years."

~ Sylvia Plath, The Unabridged Journals of Sylvia Plath

In the autumn of 2013, I skimmed along the mud flat shoals of the Red River in an airboat with four college buddies. We powered upstream through the shallow grassy sandbars pausing to shut down the engine to chat with our guide. We then headed downstream until we reached a giant dredger pulling sand from the river. We wore no seat belts, no life preservers; there wasn't a safety railing, just the wind in our hair, or in my case on my head. We did, however, don ear protection against the roar of the aft engine. We've all operated mowers, chain saws, weed eaters and tractors, sans ear protection, yet felt strangely compelled to protect our hearing against the roar of the engine and fan blades. It might be too late, like applying sun screen at midnight, but we do what we can. Sometimes we protect less vital parts of our bodies, like ears, because it's easy and convenient. But power is fickle and sometimes it reminds us of our tenuous hold on this earth.

My friend Kelly Kemp just turned fifty-five but looks forty, like he could run his college event, the 800 meters, in two minutes. Living with Kelly in Rector House at Harding University, I had seen him often in running shorts, but on this day I looked down at his thigh from my catbird perch on the air boat and saw a scar across the top of his left thigh, running side to side, a toothy serration longing to tell a story.

Saturday afternoon we sat in the living room of the Kemp's home south of Bonham, Texas, watching football games, east and west windows affording views of Texas grassland and Longhorns, the herd spiced by a lone donkey. I had forgotten about Kelly's scar, but the subject eventually arose through our meandering conversations.

Kelly and his wife Lee Ann were out near the highway on their property. Kelly was chain sawing a tree and the blade struck an adjacent metal fence post which instantly kicked the saw down to his upper thigh. Once Kelly realized the cut had not just torn his jeans, but had sliced into his thigh, he grabbed both sides of the wound and told his wife, "I'm hurt bad, call 911." They had no cell phone so Lee Ann ran to the highway and flagged down a passing car, amazingly occupied by two trained emergency responders. Upon reaching Kelly and coaxing him to take his hands off the wound, they began to care for him and when he released his hands, blood jetted high into the air. The EMT shouted, "Catch her!", as Lee Ann went all woozy. Kelly stayed calm as the EMT took his pulse and told him, "Your pulse is 48." Kelly was life-flighted to Parkland Hospital in Dallas where they cared for him. Kelly came home the next day, but just another inch and the blade would have severed the femoral artery of the inner thigh, and the story would have ended differently.

It's an illusion that time passes more quickly as we grow older. I can remember sitting in grade school watching the minute hand pass from 2:00 to 3:00, days when I was bored beyond words. Today, a week passes more quickly than that glacial hour of waiting in my youth, a time when everything I could see was in front of me. At my age more of my life is behind me than ahead, in proportions I can never know or understand, since tomorrow isn't any guarantee. We said our farewells at the Kemp home, and someone remarked that our last gathering was fifteen years ago, and if we wait another fifteen, Kelly would be seventy.

We went to church service Sunday morning with Kelly and Lee Ann in Bonham and I was thinking about time and space and our place in it and how we grasp for these moments, ephemeral holy moments, unexpected moments that make the hair stand up on the back of your neck. As we worshipped at the Bonham, Texas Church of Christ that autumn morning, I noticed a lady sitting just ahead and slightly to my right at a break between the pews, in a wheelchair, perhaps ninety years old. I looked at her profile, at her jaw jutting prominently through her translucent vanilla skin, projecting through sagging cheeks like the rock of ages. The congregation sang *Paradise Valley* acapella and I watched her jaw move like a stone through time,

"As I travel through life, with its trouble and strife, I've a glorious hope to give cheer on my way, soon my toil will be o'er, and I'll rest on that shore, where the night will be turned into day."

I couldn't hear her voice but she sang the words like she was seeing an old friend again after fifteen years. I caught myself missing the entirety of verse two watching her sing, and shamed, I sang verse three with gusto to make up for verse two. She was sitting next to a lady, her friend or perhaps her daughter, younger by what appeared to be a generation. We had spoken to the younger woman before the service began and she had told me about growing up in Edmond, Oklahoma, and I asked her if she had gone to Edmond High School. She said, "Yes", and I told her there were three high schools in Edmond now.

During the observance of communion, the lady in the wheelchair received broken bread from her friend, making a cup with her hands, collecting it and tossing it into her mouth as best she could, with all the dignity and reverence she could muster. When the juice came, the younger woman took the cup and tilted it into the mouth of the older lady, like a momma bird feeding a baby sparrow. Her mouth was wide open, probably as wide as she could make it, and she swallowed the juice like a wandering nomad swallowing rain drops in a parched desert.

We are all collectors, dealers in memory, keepers of time and space. It's really all we have. Our money doesn't travel well, our stuff gets put in dusty garages, our houses need painting, our cars break down, and our clothes go to Goodwill. But moments in time? That's the stuff we keep.

This weekend I talked to my good friends about work, children, wives and parents, and we shared our memories of college when we were young and naive. We told stories and white lies, we prayed and laughed, and we did nothing except be in each other's company, in the good graces and hands of Lee Ann who took care of us like we were kings. We ate delicious pie and cobbler, steak from the Kemp's pastures, and fresh salsa and peaches from their cupboards. For just a moment time slowed down and we peered upstream and downstream along old man river, reflecting on the good stuff. Skimming along a river like modern-day Huck Finn's, talking about our scars, looking at the stars and being thankful for our blessings.

26

Alone at Eve

"And it feels good to feel young with you, and at the same time to grow old with you. And it's all those things together at the same moment."

~ Dave Isay, *All There Is: Love Stories from Story Corps*

John F. Kennedy, C.S. Lewis, and Grace Walker Taylor all died on November 22nd. Just hours after my grandmother Grace passed on that date in 1993, my niece, Ashley Grace Taylor, was born on a Sunday morning. Her birth helped fill our sense of loss, Grace taken and Grace given. Grandma was ready to die. Her tithe check written that Saturday night, placed in her Bible like a bookmark. My father would place it in the contribution tray the next morning at church services. She lived alone for almost five years after losing her husband and friend, Ross Taylor, in March of 1989. Nine years earlier, during a procedure to clear his carotid artery, a stroke stole his ability to speak, other than grunts and gibberish, although at times he could mysteriously articulate an understandable word or phrase. He was a man who spoke only when necessary, a fact of personality exacerbated now by his loss of speech, but before that by the woman he married, Grace Walker Taylor.

Grandma Grace protected most of the broadcast frequencies in the Taylor household, commandeering conversations using her homespun wit and storytelling talent. Often referred to as "Amazing Grace and Old Rugged Ross", their roles remained the same after the stroke. Grandma still told homespun stories and Grandpa sat by her side grunting to express disagreement or shaking his head to steer her closer to resolution of her story or to the truth. I wasn't ever sure at which aim he grunted.

We remember Ross and Grace sitting in a porch swing, enjoying the cool of the evening as the Oklahoma sky refracted sunlight into softly muted peach and gold pastel, earth touching sky. Grandpa Taylor rocked the swing while twiddling his thumbs, admiring the sunset, filling his role as sounding board for the day's events, duly recounted with wit and a wink by Grandma Grace.

When two bodies become one soul, it's hard to imagine them apart. During their last nine years of marriage, my grandparents spoke as one, not just because Grandpa had lost his capacity for speech, but because they had become one soul, one voice, swinging on a porch as one and speaking in perfect unison.

Wendell Berry's poem, *"They Sit Together on the Porch"* paints the picture I have in mind of my grandparents, sitting in the swing on the back porch, gazing at the horses and cattle in the pasture. Even though it was mostly Grandma speaking, especially after the stroke, the words were of one mind.

"They sit together on the porch, the dark

Almost fallen, the house behind them dark.

Their supper done with, they have washed and dried

The dishes—only two plates now, two glasses,

Two knives, two forks, two spoons—small work for two.

She sits with her hands folded in her lap,

At rest. He smokes his pipe. They do not speak,

And when they speak at last it is to say

What each one knows the other knows.

They have one mind between them, now, that finally

For all its knowing will not exactly know

Which one goes first through the dark doorway, bidding

Goodnight, and which sits on a while alone."

-Wendell Berry

The question, what becomes of *one married soul* when the first half passes through the "dark doorway", is intriguing to me, piqued by an increasing sense of marital solitude Karen and I now experience as our children have left the nest of our home. Karen told me recently she feels a sense of selfishness about me now that the kids are gone. I have no idea what she's talking about. My response was that as a father of three, I've been number four on her list for the past twenty years. Nevertheless, over dinner last night, Karen wondered aloud about my plans to remarry in the event of her demise. I had no answer. I know the bed would never get made again in my lifetime, unless I married again. Flipping the question around, she couldn't imagine playing the dating game and marrying again. Like the brilliant Sicilian in *The Princess Bride*, it was simply inconceivable to her. And so I think about my Grandma going on with life for another fifty-six months, swinging alone, talking to the cattle, her unspoken words and those she dared to speak aloud, carried along in the Oklahoma wind to the spirit of her other half.

Ross & Grace Taylor

Grandma often told stories in ways that made you flinch or at least whisper, "Did she really say that?" Grandma often delighted in the use of a technique Anton Chekhov employed. She would say, "Ross and I often slept together before we married." This in an age that disavowed premarital euphemisms. "*Slept together*" and questionable timing sounded odd and wrong. Then she would explain, "We grew up in the same community and the families would put Ross and me into the crib together," to sleep as it were, without the scandalous innuendo. Grandma was making it strange, telling stories in fresh ways, shining light in dark places with humor and wit.

Grandma Grace had a way of making the simple things fresh in her stories, sometimes so fresh that they sound strange. Grandma Grace sitting alone in the swing seemed strange to me. It was like watching massive waves breaking on the beach without a sound, odd, absurd, incomplete. Aristotle said, "Love is composed of one soul inhabiting two bodies." The Christian and Jewish Bible says that a man leaves his parents, is united with his wife and they become one flesh. Certainly the physical connotation applies here, but does scripture also agree with Aristotle? Not so much in the literal sense that they have one soul, but in the practical sense that they begin to think the same thoughts and value the same virtues and believe the same family mythology. Are we to swing in the same swing?

I'm sure Grandpa's stroke brought to eminence the thought sometimes unspoken, but often considered, "Which one goes first through the dark doorway, bidding good night, and which sits on a while alone?" Strangely, Karen and I mention this from time to time. It's an imaginative game we play. Grandma sat on alone in the swing and since she lived next door, we often picked her up on the way to church. Surely Grandma Grace thought of her husband as the Church sang his favorite song, "*Walking Alone at Eve*".

"Sitting alone at eve and dreaming the hours away,
Watching the shadows falling now at the close of day;
God in His mercy comes with His Word He is drawing near,
Spreading His love and truth around me and everywhere."

In the car on the way back home, with her seat belt held against her side but not fastened, because…well, I don't really know why she did that…she would say in her unique way of deflecting any sense of satisfying the Bohemian lusts of the flesh, "I believe the children would enjoy a Braum's ice cream cone." And my three-year old daughter, Lauren, who struggled with her articulation of S, would yell, "Yeaahh! I want a 'coop 'n a cup 'n a 'poon!" Grandma would then say quietly, "I believe a small vanilla shake would be good for me." And the real motive would emerge craftily disguised by concern about depriving the children of ice cream. Her depression era sensibility forbade permission to ask directly for anything that could be construed as indulgent.

I know not who goes through the *dark doorway* first. Karen and I are still enjoying the swing and the sunsets. Daughter Lauren reminds me when she does something less than stellar, or perhaps remarkably strange, that the nut fell not far from the oak tree. Like her, my acorn did not stray from beneath the canopied shade of my storytelling Grandma Grace. I enjoy stories, porch swings, and ice cream.

If only I could sit beside Grandpa Ross on the porch swing listening to Grace Walker Taylor spin one more yarn. We'd listen, admire the sky, watch the cows lazily chew grass and we wouldn't have to say a word.

27

Icebergs in Cornfields

"The genius of Jesus of Nazareth is that he found the holy not among the monastic, but among the profane."

~ Reinhold Niebuhr

When Belinda Carlisle of the Go-Go's sings "Heaven is a place on earth" I stop whatever I'm doing and sing along: "Ooh baby do you know what that's worth, you make heaven a place on earth!"

It happened today, in my truck while driving to Tulsa and a blue-haired lady with a handicap sign hanging from her rear view mirror stared me down as she passed on the left. I guess my singing slows my driving and octogenarians humming Sinatra pass me.

Is Heaven revealed in common moments, unassuming revelation, like Belinda Carlisle singing about love? Is Heaven a place on earth? Not all the time, but rather in "tip of the iceberg moments" we see now and then, understanding the ice flow is mostly under the surface of the ocean, unrevealed.

Which reminds me of my favorite baseball movie, *Field of Dreams*. Ray Kinsella walked out the door of his childhood home at the age of seventeen and he never spoke to his Dad again. He tells Terrence Mann, played by James Earl Jones, "By the time I was ten, playing baseball got to be like eating vegetables or taking out the garbage. So when I was 14, I started to refuse. Could you believe that? An American boy refusing to play catch with his father."

His Dad died before they reconciled. And now, on a brilliant green baseball diamond in the midst of Iowa corn, Ray Kinsella, played by Kevin Costner, sees his Dad. As the catcher's mask comes off they have a catch as I struggle to swallow. Every time I watch that moment a baseball leaps from the screen into my throat and I can't swallow and my eyes mist over.

John Kinsella (father): Is this heaven?

Ray Kinsella: It's Iowa.

John Kinsella: Iowa? I could have sworn this was heaven.

[starts to walk away]

Ray Kinsella: Is there a heaven?

John Kinsella: Oh yeah. It's the place where dreams come true.

[Ray looks around, seeing his wife playing with their daughter on the porch]

Ray Kinsella: Maybe this is heaven.

Robert Farrar Capon likes to suggest as the image of God's providence and mercy, an iceberg. Like the mighty expanse of ice from the polar caps, the ice extends out into the ocean in all directions, and the sailors of those areas have to be on guard and alert for the tip of the icebergs where the grace of God makes a brief revelation of its power, light, and love. The iceberg seen is not all there is. Someday when the ocean is drained we may see the full extent of the ice, but for the time being all we see, if we are alert, are the iceberg tips. Those who are a part of the people of the light have to keep watch for the icebergs so that they might continue to know and to see the nature and purpose of God and to encourage each other with stories and testimonies about the icebergs.

Jesus prayed, "Thy Kingdom Come, Thy Will be done, on Earth as it is in Heaven." Perhaps he was talking about being watchful for the tip of the iceberg, a son and father having a catch, a moment swinging on the front porch with someone you love, holding your child seconds after she is revealed as not only a miracle but a miracle in which you were asked to participate, moments when the world is turned upside down and the poor become rich and the weak become strong, as Heaven breaks out on Earth.

I once thought Knute Rockne was the author of The Lord's Prayer giving football players something to say in those awkward locker room moments just before kick off when frothy violence and masculine intimacy touch and recoil. But I was wrong. It's a prayer about the intersection of Heaven and Earth, where the dirt road intersects the street of gold. And, if you have 'ears to hear' as Jesus encouraged, perhaps like Ray Kinsella you will hear voices and build ball fields in corn as high as an elephant's eye, at a four-way stop where Heaven meets Earth. It's the place where dreams come true and mountains begin to move and rivers change their course.

28

The Best Shortstop I Ever Saw

"I believe that what we become depends on what our fathers teach us at odd moments, when they aren't trying to teach us. We are formed by little scraps of wisdom."

~ Umberto Eco, *Foucault's Pendulum*

I married into a family of shortstops. I never saw my father-in-law play shortstop, but I heard the stories. A "Gatorade cooler dumped on my head" moment of clarity regarding my diminishing skills as a shortstop happened one summer evening in the hole between short and third, as I reached down across my body for a grounder and caught a bit of dirt and air turning a routine out into a single. I turned and watched that ball roll into the left field grass, carrying my confidence along with it like Terrence Mann walking into a field of corn, never to be seen again.

My diminished skills as a shortstop remind me that we all face a time of recognition. Moments we understand our mortality, our inability to bend over and scoop up a grounder in the hole, or to even take another step without pain. Thomas Emory Mason was once tall, strong, and lean, a Jersey working man. I remember sitting next to Thom at the Philadelphia Airport waiting for my wife Karen and my one-year old daughter Lauren to return from California. Thom asked to come along, to "take a ride with me" as he put it. He missed his daughter and granddaughter. We sat and talked about the Phillies, his work as a foreman at a block plant, my work as a CPA, and then he said something I'll always remember, "I'm going to die young."

Much of the skin on his legs was grafted from his back since he fell into a steam curing vat in February 1985, at the block plant where he was foreman. On June 15, 1985, Thom walked Karen down the aisle at our wedding, stubborn, proud and strong, but hobbled by skin stretched tightly into Halloween-worthy scars hidden beneath black slacks. Thom had also lost a finger and a half in another plant accident. Karen inherited his physical grace, and Thom's kids knew from whence their stumbling and bumping into things came. Thom exhibited good humor about of his shortcomings. Not long after his hand accident, at a charades game his son stuck a hand out in a celebratory way of offering a high-five and said to his father, "Hey, gimme four." And he did.

Thom's father died in his fifties, and the reality that Thom lived and worked and raised kids without rest for his entire adult life, and had smoked cigarettes for much of that time, colored his view of life expectancy. I sat and listened at the airport, didn't know what to say, mostly just listened.

He was one of the kindest and most affirming men I've known. His final year of life was filled with physical pain, but also spiritual and emotional treasures. Getting him in and out of a split level home was a chore. His son built him a trail of plywood from the front drive around to the back second floor deck and the steps were covered with a ramp. Pushing him along that plywood trail was easy, but the ramp up to the deck took all the strength I had.

I lifted him from the car one late December evening feeling the wincing pain transfer from his frail body to my arms as I helped him into a wheelchair. His pain and frailty shocked me, making me think of our airport conversation about mortality. He would die a little over a month later on February 22, 2003, at the end of a year that he considered the best of his life.

We were in Duncan, Oklahoma on a Saturday afternoon when we received word of his passing, and Monday morning we sat on a blizzard shrouded runway in Tulsa getting ready to fly into that same Philly airport where Thom and I had chatted about mortality some thirteen years earlier. I was asked to say some words at his funeral and agreed, with no idea what to say. As our jet ascended through the darkness into brilliant morning sunlight, I began writing whatever came into my mind about my father-in-law on the back of my boarding pass. I took those boarding pass notes and a legal pad and sat at the kitchen table of the Mason home for a couple of days and listened to family and friends cry, laugh, and remember. What I wrote next came easily and all at once, and I shared most of it at Thom's memorial service.

Thomas Emory Mason, Jr.

One of the wonderful qualities Thom possessed was punctuality. He was on time to a fault. The coffee pot was set before bed and he arose along with the aroma of brewing coffee at 4:30 a.m. Thom enjoyed a cup before leaving for work, but one cup wouldn't do. He rarely passed a Wawa convenience store without stopping. He once told me about driving past Wawa and his truck would signal and turn into Wawa on its own volition, like a divining rod seeking water. He was the Lone Ranger of Wawa and his Ford truck was his horse, Silver, understanding the next move without prompting.

Thom always managed time well, and in 1971, he knew it was time, time to move his family. Thom and Ann Mason moved their five children to Tabernacle, NJ and during construction of their split-level home on a pine-tree laden lot on Summit drive, they would pile into the baby blue Volkswagen van and travel south on Route 206 from Yardville, NJ, from the white clapboard house with the big owl wood carving mounted on the front gable. They left the youthful stomping grounds of Thomas Emory Mason, Jr. to go to a new place, a new home that would provide so many new cherished memories.

As they cruised Route 206, the family sang "Let there be peace on earth" and they really believed they sounded harmonious and in key. And if they caught Dad singing out loud to a country tune, the kids craftily turned down the volume and stopped singing so they could hear the unfiltered voice of their Father in full song bellowing out Merle Haggard.

Words can't speak fully of the rich tapestry of Thom's life nor how he touched those he loved. The best of what remains is what we've kept inside our hearts, our memories of Pop-Pop. So we remember…

We remember his work ethic and the pride expressed in his job and that the personal possessive applied to his stories of work. Thom would speak of *his* block plant and *his* blocks and *his* workers and *his* equipment and only *he* knew how to run that plant and manage all of its quirky issues. He liked to talk about his challenges at the plant and his victories and he made us feel like it was part of him. He talked about what he loved and putting in a good days work was part of his personality.

We remember Thom liked to eat. He once served in the Army Reserve as a cook which explains his penchant for great big pots and pans and cooking eggs and bacon and pork roll. I asked my daughter Lauren her memory of Pop-Pop and she said, "I loved it when he made me sunny-side-up eggs."

Thom had a consequence-free voracious appetite eating mountains of food while remaining slim. He once made six peanut butter and jelly sandwiches, put them on a plate and walked past his son-in-law, Tom Achey. His question to Achey seemed generous, "Do you want a PBJ sandwich?" until the response revealed his appetite and food humor. "Yea," Achey replied, to which his father-in-law replied, "Go make it yourself, everything's in the kitchen." Thom looked like Clint Eastwood and ate like John Candy.

We remember how Thom loved playing games. I grew up a shortstop. I married into a family filled with shortstops. Thought I was pretty good. I soon found out my best rank in the family as shortstop was third behind the patriarch and his daughter Karen. While watching the Phillies, he liked to explain how he would turn a single into a double...by running hard right out of the batter's box and not slowing down, sliding hard into second base. And that's how he lived. Running hard right out of the box. He described proper shortstop technique with these words, "Do it all in one motion." Late in his life he conceded high praise to his grandson Tommy Achey while watching him play softball, "He plays shortstop like I do."

There was always time to play games after work, catch five, huckle-buckle beanstalk, blind mans' bluff and the name game. And on Christmas Eve, the family played charades. Once while hiding during a game of hide-and-seek, he hid so well the kids never found him. When they gave up, he triumphantly unfolded his 6'1" frame from the top shelf of a tiny coat closet like a Slinky recoiling down a stairway. He had won. Is it any wonder that five Mason children engage life with such buoyancy and competitiveness modeled after their Dad?

We remember how Thom loved holidays and great backyard picnics with mountains of food and children running wild, softball games, horseshoes and card games and he was right in the middle of it all directing traffic, laughing, telling stories and listening. Oh how he listened! "How 'ya doin'?" was his favorite greeting, and he really meant it. He had big ears and would sit and listen if you wanted to talk, nodding his head in affirmation as he listened. He had big ears that matched his big heart.

And if he felt you were being left out, he would say something simple but directly at you like, "Whaddya think of the Phillies chances this year?", or "What do you think was the best western ever made?", as if you were somebody and the outcome depended upon your considered answer, making you the smartest person in the room at that moment.

We remember the places Thom took us. The Dixie Drive-In. Camping in Maine. Hiking up to the pinnacle of Bowman's tower at Washington's Crossing on the Delaware River.

Bowman's Tower overlooking the Delaware River near George Washington's Crossing

We remember how respected Thom was around the Tabernacle community and among his family and friends. And when he did things for you, you remembered them. Like the Valentine's Day Karen looked out her window at Northeastern Christian College and saw her Dad striding across campus to deliver a paper mache heart filled with five silver dollars. That year he gave the same gift to each of his four daughters and his daughter-in-law, Kathy, who was really like a fifth daughter to him.

Thom was a strong man who never gave up and like the movie stars he admired most, Robert Shaw and Clint Eastwood and Charles Bronson, he fought gallantly until the end. He never quit running hard around the bases of life and it was only late in his life that he realized he was no longer stretching a single into a double…he was headed home.

Sometimes beauty is magnified through the lens of pain. As Karen and I lifted off the runway in Tulsa, we left fourteen inches of snow and ice and slick roads along with brutal sullen skies. Between Tulsa and St. Louis, I looked over at Karen as she slept and then looked out the window thinking about Thomas Emory Mason. We emerged into the clear sky before daybreak. I looked out over the wing at this glorious billowing expanse of smoky gray and white clouds, spreading out to eternity like a brooding lumpy blanket. It looked like an ice mass at the North Pole, an endless mass reaching beyond sight, forever it seemed, and I watched the tip of the sun peak over the pillowy canopy to announce the dawn. Soon the sky was awash in brilliant orange streams of light announcing new life and new day. I thought about Thom and how he battled and how he didn't want to die. But he still found beauty through the pain that racked his body. He saw goodness through the prism of the disease that consumed his mortal body.

He saw the streaming morning sun through the brooding clouds. Just a month before he died he said, "This year was the best year of my life."

Jim Valvano, the basketball coach said shortly before he succumbed to cancer, "This disease can take my mortal body, my flesh, but it can't touch my mind, it can't touch my heart, and it will never touch my soul."

Thom with his daughter Karen, June 15, 1985

Late in his fight, from his bed or wheelchair, Thom would sing the first line of a song from the Seventies disco era which was never meant to be a comfort to his suffering, but he turned it on its head and made it his theme. "I believe in miracles."

I believe in miracles too.

And I believe in the providence of God.

And I believe that someday, I'll round third and head for home.

The words of the gospel of John chapter 14

"In my Father's house are many rooms; if it were not so, I would have told you. I am going there to prepare a place for you. And if I go and prepare a place for you, I will come back and take you to be with me that you also may be where I am."

Someday, I'll see Pop-Pop and he'll have a room in the Father's house. He'll invite me in and shake my hand with a five-finger handshake. His legs renewed and strong. With clear eyes and broad smile he'll greet me and give me a hug. He'll say, "Sit down, we have all day to talk about anything you want."

We'll sit and chat as a savory smell drifts from a pot of soup. He'll say, "I asked around when I got here and took a poll. I am the best shortstop in the family."

I'll smile and shake my head slowly, "No, Thom, you weren't the best shortstop in the family...you were the best I ever saw."

29

Watching the Sons of Autumn

"It's a father's duty to give his sons a fine chance."
~ George Eliot, Middlemarch

I once saw a list of things Dad's should teach their sons. How to balance a checking account, how to ask a girl out, how to change a tire, and so on. As I think about my failure to teach my son these skills, I realize how much nurturing help I've had.

Saturday I was playing golf with a group of Dads who have met annually since October 4, 1997, when we prayed prostrate under the shadow of the Washington Monument at a Promise Keepers rally, along with half a million other men gathered near the Capitol of our country. We prayed for our children, those born and unborn, and prayed for fatherly perseverance. We've met every autumn since 1997, except the year of the 9/11 attacks in 2001. We eat, laugh, and play like when we were boys. We pray for our families, reminding ourselves of the stone of remembrance we placed in our hearts near the Washington Monument that year. And just like many of our parents reminded us before we walked out the door on a Friday night, we remember who we are and whose we are, children of a just and loving Father God.

So on Saturday afternoon, I stood on the ridge of the little golf course at our home and looked east to the sun-splashed pond and watched the product of our 1997 prayers, the sons of our autumn promise. Brandon and four buddies from OU wake-boarded along the cat tails lining the banks, and my nephew Jacob swam across the pond solo while nephews Easton and Tyler swam and kayaked. Boys being boys, giddy and bullet proof, just like our generation played midnight Frisbee in our underwear and ski jumped over firewood ramps packed with snow and clothed the Community Center statue with a toga.

It's fun to see life come full circle, and yet our sons are not the same. They are unique, they have an identity all their own. Their identity is more spiritual and less religious, more egalitarian and less biased, immersed with personal devices held in the palm of their hands accessing more information than all the libraries of the world contained when we were their age. We sat in a circle around the campfire Saturday night looking at the stars through the canopy of the hackberry tree, and we talked about how this group of Dads came to meet again and again each autumn. My brother, Greg, challenged us with questions about belief and identity...Who are you? Do you judge your worth by the grades you make and the degrees you have earned? Are you eternal, or just a mist? Are you a child of God, a citizen of Heaven?

I grew up in a church that sang about heaven, a cappella, and when we sang *"Mansions Just Over the Hilltop"* the words that resonated were not the words about streets of gold, but rather the line about the prophet whose pillow was a stone. I understood that prophet, the one with no permanent dwelling, tempted, tormented and tested, wandering about with a crick in his neck from sleeping with his head on a rock. Sometimes being a dad is a pain in the neck. But I'm always looking for echoes of better days, glimpses, moments, when I peer into the future and see men who were once boys.

I've always thought of Heaven in bright colors. My theory about Heaven as a youngster included an inexhaustible bowl of peanut M&M's flowing eternally like a rainbow dotted stream tumbling down a mountain. It wasn't the stuff of Augustine, but it gave a creative flourish to my spare understanding of reward and punishment and colored my black and white Bible in brilliant Technicolor. Walking through the gates of Heaven would be like the moment in *The Wizard of Oz* when the film transitions to color, as a sepia-toned Dorothy opens the door of a Kansas farmhouse and the vibrant world of Oz explodes in lush and gorgeous Technicolor, revealing Dorothy wearing a bright blue gingham dress as she steps over the threshold in a moment of true awe, no longer constrained by black and white.

Once in a blue moon, we catch a glimpse of the Technicolor scene on the other side of the door. Saturday, with golf clubs held in our hands like the staffs of Moses and Aaron, we gazed down from our golf game on the hill and admired our sons playing in the cat tails, riding the waves on a brilliant autumn day, and we remembered the smell of the earth and grass under the shadow of a towering obelisk seventeen years ago. Thank you Lord for answering our prayers.

30

My Hand Me Down Friend

"When we honestly ask ourselves which people in our lives mean the most to us, we often find that it is those who, instead of giving advice, solutions, or cures, have chosen rather to share our pain and touch our wounds with a warm and tender hand. The friend who can be silent with us in a moment of despair or confusion, who can stay with us in an hour of grief and bereavement, who can tolerate not knowing, not curing, not healing and face with us the reality of our powerlessness, that is a friend who cares."

~ *Henri J.M. Nouwen, Out of Solitude*

I've never wanted to wear my Father's clothes, which makes this scene surreal: College kids diving after my clothes like starving refugees collecting Cinnabons. I purged my closet over the holidays, grabbing great clutches of cotton hoodies, denim jeans, flannel shirts and tossing them to the hardwood floor of our recreation room as my children, along with nephews and nieces, dove headlong laying claim to free clothing. Apparently vintage old man clothes are just as desirable as grungy Goodwill apparel.

What's going on with the younger generation and clothes? I wandered away into the fashion wilderness myself, experimenting with disco wide lapel leisure suits and four-inch heels, but I found my way home with Lacoste polo's and 501 button fly jeans. Just as I felt the world was about right, Nineties grunge arrived and I lost all hope for the future of men's fashion. And now this, kids shopping at Goodwill and begging at the closet of dumpy dad clothing. I find solace only in the money saved buying and begging for thrift grade lumpy clothing.

But there is one hand-me-down my Father offered and I've worn easily, a friend. George Johnson is twenty years my senior, four years younger than my Dad. They met in 1970 on a Campaign for Christ in Hamilton, Ontario, and have spent time together since, partnering in several businesses together and sharing beans and cornbread at countless tables. Beans and cornbread seems to suit them.

Dad tells stories of my Grandma Grace sweeping pinto beans from the cracks of drafty floor planks when the supply of vittles became scarce. Remembrance of hard times colors their friendship and their attitudes toward life and business. Just as Terrel hates throwing away scrap lumber from job sites, George, well he just hates throwing away anything, paper, peanut brittle, quiche…I was reading a report from George's office recently and noticed the back of the page displayed something irrelevant to the topic. A new idea in re-purposing paper, using it twice.

George calls my Dad "Boss", because he was his boss for a time *(he still calls Terrel boss even though it's been thirty years since Terrel signed his paycheck)*. Years ago, George's office was just a few steps down the hall from mine. Every time George walked past my office he would say something. "Hey Brent!" and while striding past, George would whack the door jamb and proceed down the hall.

After a couple of years, I happened to glance at the door jamb and it looked as if Woody Woodpecker was looking for a home. A 12 gauge gun with birdshot from close range would have done the same thing it took George three years to accomplish. Every time he walked past and whacked the jamb, the ring on his finger impressed the wood. And so that speckled and dented doorway became a signal like the notes parents create with pencil on wall noting the height of their children. I left it alone, I didn't fix it. It was our sign of friendship, evidence of past greeting, the worn patina of steps walking past and words echoing in the halls.

George caddied for me at Canterbury Country Club in Cleveland, Ohio at the 1979 United States Amateur Golf Championship. We shared a hotel room and the night before competition commenced, I sat on the bed reading a promotional magazine for the tournament published by the U.S.G.A. My playing partner the first two days would be Hal Sutton. George and I read about Hal's amateur accomplishments, including the Western Amateur Championship. He would later win the PGA Championship in 1983. It was daunting playing with someone that good, but assuring to know George was on the bag and I knew he believed in me and always supported me as a competitor. I spent time watching him compete also, as he excelled at third base in fast pitch softball leagues.

He was the Brooks Robinson of his era, often playing only twenty feet from the batter, daring them to swing away and taking away the bunt in a game often decided by a single run. Once, a batter did swing away with George playing in and the swing produced a high Baltimore chop that hit the dirt in front of the plate, bounded high over George's head prompting George to whirl, sprint back under the now descending ball, snare it with a bare hand and throw to first base in one continuous motion, retiring the batter by a half step.

George Johnson

We office in the same building now, George Johnson Appraisal on the east side of our building and Taylor Homes Group occupying the west offices just a few strides away. George will bring stray cups of coffee into my office, left over pieces of peanut brittle from Christmas or an omelette from his 7:30 breakfast meeting at the Rotary. George likes to share things and hates to see food wasted. So we eat a lot of goodies together just because if we don't, nobody else will. It's our office fraternity, FOLGEW, Fraternity of Leftover Goodies Eaten Well, and we are the charter members.

George also tells a story of a bubbly waitress who brought silverware and water for the table after taking their order and as George was about to remind her to bring crackers, from underneath her arm, like a mother hen raising a wing producing a brood of chicks, she dramatically presented her own covey of saltines and melba toast exclaiming triumphantly, "Betcha thought I forgot the crackers!" At least they were warm.

George is famous for down-home witticisms. For instance, if you ask George if he wants a piece of coconut cream pie he's likely to say, "I don't believe I don't". If the topic is what's for dinner, George says, "If we had some ham, we could have some ham and eggs, if we had some eggs," and if the mood is melancholy he might resort to, "I feel more like I do today than I did yesterday."

A few nights ago, headed home, I noticed George's office light burning. I walked down the hall, peeked in and said, "George, I'm taking off. What's on your plate tonight?" George said, "I remember when I was a kid and Mom said the Lone Ranger is on at 5:30, and I thought, no matter what happens, it's going to be a good day. Today's kind of like that. Tonight, its Oklahoma vs Oklahoma State in basketball, Bobbie's making soup and cornbread, and no matter what, it's going to be a good day."

That's my friend George in a nutshell. No matter what happens it's gonna be a good day. For George, a good day means the Lone Ranger is on later, or a softball game, or a golf match, or spending time with grandkids, or sharing a piece of pie and conversation with whomever needs a piece of pie and conversation. Sometimes for George, all you really need is to draw a deep breath of fresh air into your lungs and let it out...then, no matter what, it's going to be a good day.

Which is a fine definition of a great person, someone you can share a piece of pie with or a few words or continual whacks on the door jamb of your life, because after all, when you are around a great person, no matter what, it's going to be a good day.

31

Telling Our Stories with Both Hands

"...books always speak of other books, and every story tells a story that has already been told."

~ *Umberto Eco, Postscript to the Name of the Rose*

At the age of two, I scrambled up a ladder to the roof of the house next door and went to the highest ridge, peering out at the world like a sailor in a crow's nest. My mom helped me down, hugged me, and exercised restraint to not boot me across the yard.

My wife and I call twenty-three children our own, three born into our house, twenty born into our hearts as nieces and nephews. They bless us by calling us Uncle Bubba and Aunt Karen. Sometimes I wonder if they will ever grow up, and sometimes I don't want them to. Remembering my checkered youth helps modulate my disappointment as a dad and uncle when I see my twenty-three children indulge in creative shenanigans.

In the midst of one Thanksgiving gathering, I spied my son and his cousin, David, assembling tools, a truck, saws, and rope next to our towering elm tree which we call the mistletoe tree, intent on ridding it of the parasite mistletoe, or perhaps claiming a bough for romantic purposes. We watched from the window for a while but when my son's feet came to rest on the top step of the ladder and a rope was slung, all I could see was a noose, so I injected some fatherly wisdom into the comedy and explained to them John Donne's thought about how we reach divinity, "Reason is our Soul's left hand, Faith her right, By these we reach divinity." While my brother Toby and I used our left hand to talk them down from the tree, we prayed with our right.

Which brings me to my brother Toby's own story of misguided juvenile behavior. Toby and his friend Curtis attempted to clothe the Bartlesville Community Center statue, *Suspended Moment* (or *disrobed self-hugging humanity*), in the name of self-righteous modesty, with a bed sheet Roman toga, only to be caught and tossed into jail. They spent a few humiliating hours there until the parents bailed them out.

Sometimes I marvel that any of us graduated from high school. Which reminds me that I've had similar thoughts about my children and nieces and nephews, thinking them incorrigible and spoiled and selfish, wanting to drop kick them across the yard and tell them to sleep outside with the dog. Then I remember that me and my brothers spent most of our youth running around town with our left hand tied behind our backs.

Children nurtured within the context of families who tell and live out stories in their daily lives are more emotionally healthy than families with barren narratives, because they live with souls centered squarely between their left hand of reason and their right hand of faith. They have been told stories that ground them securely and unfurl their dreams like kites in a March breeze. Perhaps I climbed roofs and my brother dressed statues because we were longing to display our unfettered kites as expressions of our passion and faith, outside the guiding context of reason.

Dad tells a story about reason and calm in the midst of trouble. My Dad's dad, Grandpa Ross was on the school board when there was a pie supper to raise money for the school at Bluejacket, Oklahoma. One of the patrons, drunk and bidding on every pie despite having no money, was a physically imposing man, while Grandpa Ross stood all of five foot six inches tall. Taking the drunken bull by the horns in his gentle way, Grandpa Ross walked over to the man and whispered in his ear, then took him by the arm and escorted him out of the assembly. Years later my Dad asked Grandpa Ross what he said to the man. Grandpa answered, "Don't you think I should take you home?" Nothing magical, nothing profound, nothing threatening, just good ole' common horse sense, something Grandpa Ross had in abundance. Dad was always proud to tell anyone who asked, "I'm Ross Taylor's boy."

Our children want true and noble stories filled with magic, even when they aren't. We long to have a holy genesis, a storied journey unmarred by scandal and questionable reputation. We long to tell others that we are the sons and daughters of parents who stand for something righteous and good, sons and daughters of parents who fed them stories in the evenings at the table of their youth and just wanted to know that what they saw and heard and watched was true.

Thanksgiving 2013 we packed twenty of our family around tables covered with rich food and remarkable legacy and we told the old stories of our country and the pilgrims and the harvest. We ate sweet potatoes and kale with gravy and turkey and we explored our mythological DNA as we embraced the idea that memory is what we are and if we forget who we are we are nobody. Without memory we cease to exist and would still be climbing on roofs and adorning statues in a mad dash to experience the world without a framework of understanding, and my nephew Jacob would have no reason to tell tales and say, "My name is Jacob, I'm Greg and Jill Taylor's boy."

All of us precocious roof climbers and statue clothiers who once clasped mischief against our chests like children trapping dollar bills in a swirling money machine with one hand tied behind our backs, we can now stand proudly and watch our twenty-three kids, the same ones who once drove us to distraction, and say with both hands extended in blessing, "These are my children and I am well pleased."

32

A Family of Two Dollar Bills

...kisses are a far better fate than wisdom
lady i swear by all flowers. Don't cry
--the best gesture of my brain is less than
your eyelids' flutter which says
we are for each other: then
laugh, leaning back in my arms
for life's not a paragraph
And death i think is no parenthesis"
— *E.E. Cummings*

I married into a family of seven Toms. My father-in-law, two brothers-in-law, two nephews, one son of a nephew, and a husband of a cousin, all named Tom. It's fitting then, that my daughter will soon marry Thomas Beck Martin. Toms are ubiquitous in our family so it seems strange to me that a $2 bill is somewhat rare...and that $2 bills are referred to by collectors as Toms. (Tom Jefferson graces the front of the bill)

John Bennardo, producer and director of a film called "The $2 Bill Documentary," says that when the $2 bill was first printed in 1862, "...our country did not have much wealth, and a lot of things cost less than a dollar. So the $2 bill really didn't have much of a practical use."

It became the perfect note for some rather nefarious purposes. "Politicians used to be known for bribing people for votes, and they would give them a $2 bill, so if you had one it meant that perhaps you'd been bribed by a politician," Bennardo says. "Prostitution back in the day was $2 for a trick, so if you were spending $2 bills it might get you into trouble with your wife. $2 is the standard bet at a race track, so if you were betting $2 and you won, you might get a bunch of $2 bills back and that would show that you were gambling."

The Tom got kind of a dirty rep, and over the years as inflation brought the value of the single and the two closer together it became even less necessary. Folks didn't see much use for poor ol' Tom, and in 1966 the government decided to stop making it. Ten years went by with no twos.

In 1976, the Treasury decided it would take another shot at the $2 bill. It would order the Bureau to print a special bill for the country's bicentennial, with a big picture of the signing of the Declaration of Independence on the back.

My brother-in-law, Tom Achey, came of age during the Nixon, Ford, and Carter administrations. He still has the same haircut from 1976. And something else from 1976 that he recovered just last week.

He went to buy cigarettes at a local store and was handed change. As he walked out, he glanced down at a $2 bill. There was writing on it.

Debbie   Summit   268-0642

He looked closer and saw the year, 1976. It looked like his writing. Tom had met a pretty blonde in 1976, and asked for her name and phone number and street address. He married her. Forty years later, they still are married and live in the same town in New Jersey.

Debbie Achey told her husband that it was a sign, that it was meant to be, that they met in 1976 aided by a note scribbled by Tom on a Tom, a note that somehow found it's way back home after forty years. Tom had a simpler answer, "God is telling me it's ok to smoke."

Tom saw his wife to be forty years ago and wrote her name on a $2 post-it-note. Like a homing pigeon returning to roost, one of a billion two dollar bills in circulation returned to Tom who had scribbled "Debbie   Summit   268-0642"

What happened to Summit? The house on a dirt road without an address number, only a street name, was later given the number 60, and a paved road now fronts the home of Debbie Mason Achey's youth. Debbie's mom sold the home a couple of days ago to a nice couple with a boy. His name is Mason.

And now Mason will roam the same halls of 60 Summit Drive which holds 45 years of memory for a family of Mason's, many called Tom. And the patriarch, Thom Mason, looking down knowingly, perhaps planted the $2 bill, and the kid named Mason. It makes one stop and think…and pay attention to the currency of your life.

33

A Thousand Pines

"When I went to first grade and the other children said that their fathers were farmers, I simply didn't believe them. I agreed in order to be polite, but in my heart I knew that those men were impostors, as farmers and as fathers, too…To really believe that others even existed in either category was to break the First Commandment."
— Jane Smiley, *A Thousand Acres*

He can tell a story better than Mark Twain on a riverboat drinking whiskey in the moonlight, although the surreal and the absurd are difficult to distinguish from reality. I hang near him at family gatherings, because I'm a writer and he gives me stuff you can't make up. And like Seinfeld's blonde girlfriend who can get away with anything because she is beautiful, Tom gets away with things because he is funny.

Although sometimes the story takes the storyteller to the woodshed and what emerges can't be fabricated, but only told, and it happens in the warp time of a single sentence. Tom's extemporaneous fabrication that accelerated him into warp story mode, was molded by a moment of need and suddenly, he is in a Learjet with Jamie Moyer and the Vice-President of Fox News. The twisted moment vaulted Tom from airport mundane to jet set surreal as he uttered these words to the airline reservations attendant, "You don't understand…"

It began with a white lie meant to get him to San Diego for his grandson's 1st birthday and to remain in the good graces of his wife. The lady at the counter said, "Your plane is delayed for at least three hours and there are no alternative flights," which meant most likely the next day. He was only planning to be there two days. "You don't understand," he exclaimed with the passion of a Phillies fan booing Santa Claus. "I've got to get to San Diego…my, umm, daughter is getting married at Moonlight Beach tonight at 9:00 o'clock."

He had dropped his wife at the airport early Friday morning and she was flying alone. She was not happy because he told her he had to work and couldn't make it for the birthday party. "This is a big event, a big deal, our grandchild's first birthday, and you should be there." she reprimanded. He didn't tell her that he was booked on a flight leaving at 5:00 pm EST that same Friday and arriving in San Diego at 8:00 PST.

"Do you have any proof that your daughter is getting married?" the airline clerk asked. Tom said, "Yea, I brought my wife in here this morning. She's flying out for the wedding." She typed her name into her terminal and confirmed the flight that morning. "Let me check something," and she began typing again. "Look, don't tell anyone I did this, but take this boarding pass to gate 14 and they'll take it from there."

Tom took the boarding pass to gate 14 and was quickly boarded onto a Learjet. He sat down, glanced across the aisle and saw Jamie Moyer. Tom said, "Aren't you Jamie Moyer?" Moyer replied, "Yes, I've been in Philadelphia an entire week and you are the first one to recognize me or at least say something." Tom has been a Phillies fan since childhood so they chatted and talked baseball...and weddings at Moonlight Beach and Moyer bought Tom a drink. Then everyone on the jet knew the mission...get Tom to Moonlight Beach by 9:00 pm. In the meantime, they talked and drinks were hoisted for Tom in honor of his father-of-the-bride moment.

In the meantime, the Vice-President of Fox News chatted with Tom. He told him that he had received a $2 bill as change at the grocery and on it was the name of his wife and her phone number and address from forty years ago, which he had scribbled on the $2 bill as a memo to ask her on a date. Which is exactly what the VP of Fox News was looking for, human interest stories, since most news today is filled with tragedy. They exchanged information.

They were on the ground at 8:30 and exited the plane. The VP stood chatting with Tom and said, "I'll take you to Moonlight Beach." Tom replied, "That's ok, my son is coming for me." The VP said, "OK, I'll wait here with you to make sure and if he doesn't come, then I'll take you. Don't you have a tuxedo?" "Ummm, yea, my son is bringing it, he's in the wedding also." They waited awkwardly, but then Jimmy arrived.

Tom's son drove up in a jeep, wearing shorts, flip flops, and no shirt. "Hey Pop!, he said. The Fox guy says, "No tux?" Tom replied, "He's a surfer!" The TV exec waved as they drove away. No word yet on the Fox News special about the New Jersey couple and the $2 bill.

Tom did walk his daughter down the aisle at her wedding a few weeks later, in the pines of New Jersey far far away from Moonlight Beach. He danced that evening with his daughter while wearing sunglasses and his wife snuck up behind him and removed the sunglasses to reveal the Moonlight Beach Dad was emotional?

One can never tell where a story will lead and what will be revealed in a moment of twisted story logic shaped by a Dad's love. Sometimes, "You don't understand…", is the best we can come up with. Sometimes, "You don't understand," is surreal with twists and turns of Learjets and moonlit beaches, while other times it's as clear and refreshing as friends and family and pine trees. Sometimes the pines look like a thousand people through the lense of Ray Bans and moist eyes which seems funny yet real, like Tom's stories, a thousand pine trees waving and clapping for the funny guy dancing with his lovely daughter in the evening shadows wearing Ray Bans, and he isn't telling a story, he's living it.

Tom & Megan

34

Dancing with Lauren Martin

"He had been searching for it his entire life. He had devoted himself to poetry to find it. Now, in the middle of his life, he found it. It was in the face of the love of his life, his daughter. She who had never blushed before, now blushed. And in that blushing, he knew, was the existence of God. That was the day her father learned what God was. God was pure beauty, God was his daughter's face when she blushed."
— Roman Payne

I told everyone that I would not cry and I did not. But that was my brave face in front of friends and family. It was a long walk down the aisle, about 100 yards from the garden to the wedding tree. Lauren and I chatted as we strolled toward our family and friends, but then emotion slammed into me like a freight train as I came near many beloved faces. What a beautiful place, the wildflowers Beck helped me sow and water, the wedding tree, my wife looking gorgeous, my son and daughter standing in places of honor, and my brother Greg the preacher waiting at the end of the aisle along with a young man waiting to take the hand and heart of my daughter.

I never once stressed or worried about this moment, the moment as a Dad when my legs might turn to jelly as I walked my daughter and gave her away. I did worry about the Father/Daughter dance afterward, because I don't dance well. So Lauren and I stood in the garden alone after the bridesmaids had started their walk and I said, "Let's dance". And so we did, for thirty seconds, we danced in the garden alone. I knew Lauren was going to be ok, she was in good hands, not just with a young man who loved her, but in God's hands. And so I danced with the ease of a Father who can do nothing more, except pray and love Beck and Lauren, and get out of the way.

God said to Abraham, go to a land that I will show you and your children will be too many to count, like stars or sand. I looked at the flowers we planted and watered and realized that one day the seeds of our families will be more numerous than a thousand flowers.

We sat on the front row and watched Beck gaze at Lauren, perhaps because the angle was better, but maybe because he never seemed to look away from her, like he had seen the face of pure beauty. And I knew it was over for me, I was no longer Dad in the way I was before, the one she always counted on. It was him now. And it was ok.

So four parents surrounded them and I said to Lauren and Beck, "May your marriage be filled with joy and passion, may your best dances be on kitchen floors with pasta boiling over, may righteousness blow like fresh wind stirring the flowing locks of many children, may your romantic gazes be steady and everlasting, your longing for each other a taste of your eternal relationship with God, and may your happiness flow like a river until you sit on the porch getting old realizing that you would do it all over again."

I'll always remember the dance in the garden alone with my daughter. We danced later in front of everyone near the pool and we didn't fall in, and it was good. Later we sang and danced on the deck to the song, "You make me want to shout!" The words and weight of all our lovely friends brought down the house…and the deck…the ledger board of the wood deck snapped and the dance floor sagged under the weight of celebration. That dance was good also. It's the one everybody will talk about, "Remember when Beck and Lauren got married and we brought down the deck?"

But like Mary treasuring moments in her heart, I'll always hold close the memory of a short impromptu dance in the garden with a beautiful young lady, who has a new name and husband, but will always be my lovely daughter. Thanks for dancing with me Lauren Nuk Nuk Peanut Noodles Martin, I love you!

35

Becoming Myself

"I never change, I simply become more myself."
~ Joyce Carol Oates, Solstice

Give me yourself and in exchange I will give you Myself. My will, shall become your will. My heart, shall become your heart."
~ C.S. Lewis, Mere Christianity

This morning, over coffee and my digital newspaper, I caught the image of a spider on my shirt at the upper right breast area and I brushed it off but it didn't move. It was a Ralph Lauren horse logo. My shirt was inside out. This would have bothered me in my early years before I became myself. Now it's just normal stuff. I do screwy stuff all the time and it's ok. And it reminds me of a teacher who taught me it was ok and a friend from high school that I never really knew until I was grafted into Mrs. Smith's Family Living class and we became a brother and sister.

My word was "Breech baby." We were going around the room in our Family Living class taught by Mrs. Sue Smith and we each had a turn defining a word or phrase from a list of items that we were to be tested over. And I could think of nothing but a bikini. Even though I was able to define breech baby, I offered the alternative definition when my turn came. I said, "Breech baby – a beautiful girl in a bikini". And it brought the house down.

It was a moment in the sanctuary that was her classroom. I thought little of it at the time. But later on in my life, I realized it was the moment I came of age. Not that I somehow magically changed and became another person, but the moment I realized I was ok. That people weren't secretly making fun of me, and that people might even laugh with me, not at me, and that the standard definition isn't always the right answer.

Mrs. Smith seemed to be everyone's favorite teacher. There was something about her classroom that made it ok to be irreverent, silly, to wear your shirt inside out so that the spiders were in view, and to understand and know people beyond your tight circle of friends. I don't remember ever speaking to Carol Lynn Creel before I became her "little brother" in Mrs. Smith's class. She was beautiful and a pom girl and I was the golfer with unkempt hair and Sansa-belt slacks who sometimes wore a shirt inside out not on purpose. But somehow we became friends inside the refuge of Sue Smith's class.

I've had lot's of great teachers. Some are hard and great and some are easy and great. Mrs. Smith was easy and great, not because she didn't expect our best academically, she did. But rather, she was easy in the sense that you could become yourself without trying. She was in the business of teaching her students to become not some phony conception of what their friends wanted them to be, or their parents expected them to be or authority figures coerced them to be, but rather themselves.

Later in life I read Soren Kierkegaard's quote, "Now with God's help, I shall become myself," and realize that God used angels and mentors and teachers to do this very thing.

Sue Smith was an angel, a mentor, and a teacher doing God's bidding, in helping students become themselves. I felt at home in my skin inside her classroom. That's why her students loved her so, because she made great cookies, and hosted great parties, and loved her husband Virgil, and she laughed at our bad jokes without prejudice, out loud and with great affection.

I spoke with Mrs. Smith a few times after graduation. I wish I had told her what she meant to me, about how she was respected and loved. I hope she knows I love her. She was an angel, a mentor, a lover of life and corny jokes, and even though she's gone now, she lives in each of her students who were lucky enough to call her teacher.

36

Digging in the Dirt

"One should always be drunk. That's all that matters...But with what? With wine, with poetry, or with virtue, as you choose. But get drunk."

~ *Charles Baudelaire*

Don't drink too much wine. That cheapens your life. Drink the Spirit of God, huge draughts of him. Sing hymns instead of drinking songs! Sing songs from your heart to Christ. Sing praises over everything, any excuse for a song to God the Father in the name of our Master, Jesus Christ. Ephesians 5:18-20

While playing golf recently, someone asked if I was playing my little home golf course. I said, "No, I just take care of it, mow it, water it, kind of like a garden, a hobby. Just like my wife Karen, who works in her garden beside the 8th tee box. We work together at different passions but they both involve sweat and lots of looking at the ground, into the dirt, at it's soul, it's barrenness, it's fertility.

What is it inside our nature to get our hands dirty, to dig in the dirt, to look down like stubborn mules on a plow team? Is it the same urge that causes our necks to swivel toward the stars? We look up for inspiration, we look down at aspiration. We look at the night sky in wonder and we look down in the dirt with sweat-dripping determination.

According to David Brooks in his book, "Recently, I've been thinking about the difference between the résumé virtues and the eulogy virtues. The résumé virtues are the ones you list on your résumé, the skills that you bring to the job market and that contribute to external success. The eulogy virtues are deeper. They're the virtues that get talked about at your funeral, the ones that exist at the core of your being — whether you are kind, brave, honest or faithful; what kind of relationships you formed. Most of us would say that the eulogy virtues are more important than the résumé virtues, but I confess that for long stretches of my life I've spent more time thinking about the latter than the former. Our education system is certainly oriented around the résumé virtues more than the eulogy ones. Public conversation is, too — the self-help tips in magazines, the nonfiction best-sellers. Most of us have clearer strategies for how to achieve career success than we do for how to develop a profound character."

This swiveling of our necks up and down is the struggle between our résumé nature that wants to plant and grow wonderful things in the earth, and our eulogy nature that seeks to plant and grow transcendence, a reaching upward beyond our known world to a world of hope and possibility.

So much of what we see looking down with sweat on our brow is grace and truth, the garden in the tilled soil. What we look for in the dirt nourishes us, vegetables and flowers, grace and peace, a crop of hope.

What we gaze up at in the still of the evening is that which is very close to God, planted in toil in the garden. In an amazing reversal, we look down through our garden Hubble telescope and find the organic growing of our hearts which tells us what God is like, a master gardener growing people closer to His invisible wonder, which gives us pause and moments of upward gazing at what we might one day be.

John 1:17 The law was given through Moses, but grace and truth came through Jesus Christ. 18 No one has ever seen God. But God the only Son is very close to the Father, and he has shown us what God is like.

37

Table in the Son

Falstaff: *"I will not lend thee a penny"*

Pistol: *"Why then the world's mine oyster / Which I with sword will open."*

~ *William Shakespeare, "The Merry Wives of Windsor"*

When you are young and the world is your oyster, older folks are wont to lend wisdom thus rendering the use of swords to open the sublime stubborn shell, rather useless. As if allowing youngsters to pry open oysters in search of a beautiful pearl is beyond their ability and to wield sharp objects to crack open a shell might be better left in the hands of the experienced oyster crackers.

My son, Brandon, was preparing to leave for a seven months stay at the University of Hamburg, Germany in the Meteorological Exchange Program of Oklahoma University. His coursework was to be presented in the German language. As we dined in my parents sun room at a tabelle in die son (table in the sun) with several experienced travelers who had been to Hamburg, I listened with interest to the comments and advice offered to my son. Here are some examples:

- Someone asked if I knew what was in the middle of Hamburg? I thought it was a pickle. But, apparently it's a lake called Aussenalster, which means "Pass me a pretzel" in Deutsch.

- Beer is akin to water and the children drink it because it's alcohol content is less than 2 point.

- Americans eat 12 billion more hamburgers annually than the Germans who founded the city of Hamburg. The Germans fill the hamburger void with pretzels which are abundantly subsidized and distributed by beer makers to make Germans thirst for more beer, as if they need help.

- Beethoven was deaf and couldn't even hear a subwoofer playing Metallica if he put his ear next to the woof, and he still came up with the Fifth Dimension Symphony, "I Didn't Get to Sleep at All Last Night."

- One lady who traveled and lived extensively in Germany mentioned that she always listed on applications, "Fast" under Race, and "Good" under Sex. And another time, frustrated with the need to reveal such personal information, she listed her entire family tree of ethnicity, "French Huguenot Germanic Hungarian Austrian Danish English American Indian and Just American."

- The conversation meandered into the realm of Bavarian milking cows and it was determined that everyone at the table had milked a cow, except Brandon. One gentleman regaled us with his legend of holding firm to the cows teats, and that was what made him such a good wrestler in high school, the tenacious experience of locking onto the teats and not letting go, which I found to be udderly fascinating, although not particularly useful as travel advice.

Brandon Taylor

This is the sort of counsel you get when you tell someone you are going abroad and it struck me bemusedly as a waste of breath. A young man will quickly forget the counsel of the seasoned, who attained their own independence and cultural intelligence years earlier through the systematic disregard of their elders. I told my son to carefully weigh advice given by anyone who claims to have been in Hitler's bunker when he ended it all by drinking a finger of dark Munich malt lager before ending his misery with a Luger to the temple.

And so my son went to Germany, with prayers and blessings and well-meaning advice. He learned Thermodynamics from techno-smart geeky Germans while enjoying the efficiency of the Germans just like Eisenhower who admired the Germans better angels. Ike returned from Europe after World War II with Autobahn envy and spent ten trillion dollars building Interstate 40 and it's still under construction. Anyway, I abschweifen die thema. Back to the point.

Brandon spent three months learning the language, then four months going to classes in Meteorology. Our family traveled there to see him and to see Germany with our own eyes. Flying from Washington D.C. to Frankfurt on Lufthansa, I watched the Salzburg choir and symphony perform a majestic piece by Bach and was reminded of an illuminating scene from the television series, *Band of Brothers,* illustrating how horror and beauty inhabit the same landscape.

American paratroopers of the 101st airborne are sitting in the bombed out shell of a building observing three German men play an achingly gorgeous concerto and one remarks about how those Germans sure can play Bach to which Captain Nixon rebuts, "That's not Bach, that's Beethoven." The next day while patrolling the woods near the town from which this gorgeous music was played, the Americans discovered a concentration camp. From the mind of one nation comes beauty and horror, from the mind of one person, angels and demons.

Sitting next to us on our flight, we met a German from Dresden. He's works as an Information Technology professional. He showed my wife how to pause her movie, "The Hunger Games," so she could eat her brownies covered with strawberries and whipped cream. I asked him about the fire bombings of Dresden during World War II. He said the core of his city was totally flattened. Nice guy. Germans seem much more friendly than in movies like "Where Eagles Dare."

We visited Rothenberg during our vacation in Germany, dubbed the "most German of German" cities by Hitler, sun-drenched pastel walls were once targeted by allied bombers before they were called off in the name of historical preservation. The city's beauty reminds me of a paragraph written by George Eliot in her book *Middlemarch*, which describes simple unadorned beauty in Miss Brooke against those who put on beauty as if it is a costume to wear hiding the interior reality. "Miss Brooke had the kind of beauty which seems to be thrown into relief by poor dress. Her hand and wrist were so finely formed that she could wear sleeves not less bare of style than those in which the Blessed Virgin appeared to Italian painters; and her profile as well as her stature and bearing seemed to gain the more dignity from her plain garments, which by the side of provincial fashion gave her the impressiveness of a fine quotation from the Bible."

That's how I felt walking the cobblestones of Rothenberg watching young artists gaze at tower clocks, giant pencil sketch pad in their laps drawing shape, shadow, contour, dimension, perspective, beauty, in a place dripping with form. This is the sort of beauty Walt Disney tried to capture in theme parks and cartoons, but this beauty can only be chiseled from the stone of time.

Outside these old walls and beyond the moat that is still filled with dry grass and a small trickle of water is the modern city of Rothenberg. The new city began leaving the old city behind four hundred years ago in favor of function and enlightenment. The shrink-wrap moment that preserved old Rothenberg in a time warp was aided by the conversion of the entire town from Catholicism to Protestant Lutheranism, bringing the military might of Rome down on them and the Thirty Years War, as well as the Black Plague, events leaving this town stunted economically, socially, politically, stripped of every adornment of progress and left with only the unadorned beauty of what once was, when this city on a hill was an independent city/state and one of the finest cities in Europe.

From the ashes of World War II bombings, from the human folly and religious certitude of the Thirty Years War, from the festering boils of the Black Plague, rose beauty. Rothenberg is simple, old, and remarkably beautiful.

The longing we have for the old ways, the simple, everlasting time-tested beauty of place is all that's left now. Folks come from all over God's earth to see it after all these years, still here, set in stark relief to autobahn speed, modernism and slick temporal skin-deep beauty, an ancient German city set in relief by poor dress, like a fine quotation from the bible.

I wonder how the advice given at the table on that day before my son left for Germany compared to the actual experience of his visit. People seem to give advice because it affirms what they've discovered inside the shell of their lives and perhaps it gives them comfort. In Germany, you see your own humanity as if looking in a mirror, your own goodness and brokenness is an echo resounding against the mountains. In Germany we found beer with pretzels and a side of addiction, Beethoven weeping to the strains of the final solution, and a lovely old city on a hill risen from the ashes of plague, religious persecution, and B-17 bombings, beauty framing the angels of darkness. Sometimes it takes a visit to another country to see our own flaws and our own loveliness, a picture of ourselves as we truly are.

We are in the end, however, free moral agents who find our way without the counsel of the wicked and the good, and in the spirit of Shakespeare's Pistol, we discover what is inside our soul on our own, an oyster of hope or something less, using our sword as a malicious weapon or as a lovely tool.

Bombing ruins Rothenberg old city

38

His Folgers Can is Empty

'I've learned that people will forget what you said, people will forget what you did, but people will never forget how you made them feel.'

~ *Maya Angelou*

The man with the shepherd crook disguised as a dust mop has died. There is a melancholy in the closet where the mops lean against the wall and the Folger's can is empty, no longer filled with Brach's candy. Rusty gave it all away.

General Douglass MacArthur said, "Old soldiers never die; they just fade away," except for one soldier in my youth who will never fade. Albert "Rusty" Matthews was a war hero, unbeknownst to me. I knew him as the custodian, the guy with candy who knew my name and treated me as if I was worthy of a grown up conversation although I was only ten years old. His office was a supply closet scented with pine cleaner. He was a guidance counselor in janitor clothing, counseling the shy and socially disconnected in a school hallway with a dust mop and pockets filled with hard candy waiting for an orphaned moment of childhood insecurity.

So many children loved Rusty. We knew so little about Mr. Matthews, except he loved us and watched out for the lost children, the quiet ones, the castaways, the unpopular. He didn't have an MBA, but he was a police officer, a lumber man, a janitor, a decorated war hero. My daughter recently asked about furthering her education and I told her a few things about getting an MBA degree, but I wish I had told her this.

Be like Rusty. Live your life with a sense of wonder, a gleam in your eye, and candy in your pocket. Love the gentle, the shy, the broken, the hurting. Do the menial, the necessary, the dutiful, and when you are able, the heroic. But mostly polish floors and sweep away dirt and shine your life with gems of friendship, hard work, and a reputation beyond reproach. And then people will judge you for who you are, not by what hangs framed on your wall. Get a long handle dust mop to guide lost sheep while you work, a generous pocket of candy, and speak with those who don't know how to talk yet...those things are hard to frame and hang on a wall...but immeasurably more valuable than any degree.

Rusty, we'll miss you old soldier, sweeper of floors, watcher over children. You will never fade away.

Albert "Rusty" Matthews

39

Hiking with Elijah

The LORD said to Elijah, "Go, stand in front of me on the mountain, and I will pass by you." Then a very strong wind blew until it caused the mountains to fall apart and large rocks to break in front of the LORD . But the LORD was not in the wind. After the wind, there was an earthquake, but the LORD was not in the earthquake. After the earthquake, there was a fire, but the LORD was not in the fire. After the fire, there was a quiet, gentle sound. When Elijah heard it, he covered his face with his coat and went out and stood at the entrance to the cave.

Then a voice said to him, "Elijah! Why are you here?" I Kings 19:11-13

Abraham Joshua Heschel said, "I did not ask for success; I asked for wonder." Wonder is one of the reasons I stare at constellations, marvel at newborn babes, and hike with my son. We have hiked many miles over the years.

The best part of hiking has always been wondering what's around the next boulder or switch back. Just ahead is a stream, beyond that a bluff, a bear smells us, then we see the bear and we stare at one another with no deferential etiquette, just unabated staring bear to man and man to bear. Then a stone chimney rises like a story begging to be told before it falls ingloriously into the humus, and a fence made with the same stone marks the land, once coveted and now abandoned.

Stories rise from the dirt mingling with campfire smoke as we tune in to the small space of earth we explore under the canopy of our immense universe. These patches of earth we walk are exalted places to discover as the immaculate artist reaches down to share light and shading, texture and color, with common dumbfounded witnesses.

Hiking gives way to wonder accompanied by the naming of the wonder using words, but sometimes, only silence is worthy of the moment. Hiking is also about the unexpected gift, often wrapped in competing emotions, converging lasers of bliss and despair pointing to what you already know but won't say out loud.

This summer while hiking in New York with my wife Karen and daughter Jenna, a story emerged from the dense canopied forest and I realized that I was not only a character in the story, but also the audience. I experienced the gift of recognition, the vision of a different path, what my life might look like if a foot slipped instead of holding firm. In the midst of my emotional frenzy I hit bottom, no really, I hit my bottom, as my favorite white summer shorts slid into the hillside like Prince Fielder sliding into second turning a triple into a double. This scar, this hiking stain at my back pocket is courtesy of an ancient gorge cut into a wooded hill south of Ithaca, NY. But it's the other mark, the stain left on my spirit as I walked down an alternate trail, that won't wash away.

We were on our way to a wedding in upstate New York. My wife Karen, along with our three children, ages 25, 23, and 22, along with my daughter's boyfriend, were meandering on a road trip that brought us a few miles south of Cornell University, an area referred to by the Chamber of Commerce pun , "Ithaca is Gorges."

Determined to avoid a Comfort Inn breakfast bar vacation, we consulted Trip Advisor and booked a yurt, a round tent, surrounded by an organic garden of lettuces, cilantro, peppers, and herbs. Michelle checked us in. She was pretty in an earthy way like her vegetables, organic and natural, no makeup, what I would have called a hippie thirty years ago, but now she rents a round tent in her backyard garden to supplement her career as a realtor. Michelle described the gorge several hundred yards behind the yurt. "You can walk back to the falls, you'll hear the roar, but there are no distinct trails like in public parks, so be careful."

Our Yurt in New York

While Lauren, Beck, and Brandon drove to the Syracuse airport to pick up Brandon's girlfriend, Elizabeth, we settled in and explored the garden and set up the kitchen preparing for a dinner of pasta, Italian sausage, and a fresh salad from the garden just outside our door. Karen, Jenna, and I, wandered the grounds, exploring the chicken pen with several dozen laying hens. There was a manicured path along the boundary of the woods and a meadow stood between us and the forest which hid the waterfall.

We walked along the path to the edge of towering spruce and pine. Underneath the treed canopy we entered a gentle world, softly lit, unplugged. A thick layer of evergreen needles, leaves, and humus kept growth to a minimum. The forest floor sprouted only an occasional mushroom or an ambitious vine that had stolen enough sun to make a life. So the walking was easy initially, footing was sure until we started down the steep hill toward the roar of the gorge as the earth became more suspect, slick with water trickling just underneath the top layer of rotting leaves and needles.

We walked until we heard the sound of water cascading in the gorge just fifty yards down the hill, but still unseen. Karen's competitive nature propelled her down the hillside while Jenna and I hung back watching her traverse and disappear. I was carrying a mug of coffee, walking in my favorite Sanuk beach bum slip-ons, unprepared for a jaunt down a steep ravine on unstable compost. She was gone. I turned and looked at Jenna and we waited. By this time, I had set my coffee mug against a tree and given up on keeping my shoes free of mud. I was worried and set off down the gorge hoping to see the entire bottom of the gorge from my perch thirty feet above, but I could only see half of the stream bed on the other side. And I began to wonder if Karen had slipped and fallen into the gorge. I walked up to Jenna and told her to run back. Check the yurt. If she isn't there, go get help.

Then I turned and slipped down the muddy hill all the way to a place where I was able to drop myself to the rock stream bed worn smooth by constant flowing water. I waded downstream toward the falls filled with dread, a vision of Karen lying sprawled in a heap, hurt badly, maybe worse. I was walking down a trail I never had walked down before and I began to think, "What would I do without her?"

Hiking for me had always been about the wonder of what was just around the bend, but now, just around the bend meant my life might change instantly, and I prayed that it wouldn't, that just around the bend would be mundane and uninteresting, water, rock, soil, vegetation.

I saw nothing. I scrambled up the bank and began climbing crab-like, feet splayed, a billy-goat on all fours. It was the only way to not fall back down into the gorge.

Reaching the top, I heard Jenna calling me. But I couldn't make out her words over the roar of the water. She came closer and Karen was behind her. Karen had somehow circled back through the trees and gone back to the yurt, oblivious to our search. When Jenna saw Karen in the garden, she cried and hugged her. When I saw Karen, I said something dull-witted that I can't remember, and began walking back toward the meadow. We had walked about a hundred yards and I turned around and said feebly, "Don't do that again." And I hugged her.

I had walked down a trail unprepared, in surfer shoes and summer shorts, filled with uncertainty, dread, fear. And yet somehow, I realized it was a gift. The gift of a different kind of wonder. The gift of seeing myself walking down a different road and understanding there are no guarantees in this world. The wonder is that we are here at all. It makes me think of an exchange in one of Charles Portis' books. A church woman engages the protagonist in a discussion about eternal reward and damnation, heaven and hell. "Isn't it strange that people would be walking about in heaven and hell?" To which came the reply, "Is it not strange that we are walking about here on earth?"

Indeed, sometimes it is strange to be walking about on this earth unsure of what is around the next bend on the trail. But that dynamic tension is what makes our lives worth living, and if we are unaware of the absurdity and beauty that we see side by side on our hike, we become deaf and blind.

Hiking makes me think of Elijah in the Bible. The Lord said,

"Go out and stand on the mountain in the presence of the Lord, for the Lord is about to pass by. Then a great and powerful wind tore the mountains apart and shattered the rocks before the Lord, but the Lord was not in the wind. After the wind there was an earthquake, but the Lord was not in the earthquake. After the earthquake came a fire, but the Lord was not in the fire. And after the fire came a gentle whisper. When Elijah heard it, he pulled his cloak over his face and went out and stood at the mouth of the cave."

Here's to hiking like Elijah through a swirl of brilliant dancing leaves watching heaven touch earth in wondrous moments, at a place where the holy intersects our sodden wanderings.

40

All the Laughs on Your Side

"I love people who make me laugh. I honestly think it's the thing I like most, to laugh. It cures a multitude of ills. It's probably the most important thing in a person." — *Audrey Hepburn*

"Do you have time to come home and help Dad? He fell and broke his leg." Well, yes Mom, since you put it that way, I think I can find the time. And thanks for phrasing it in a non-urgent way so as not to alarm me and also give me an out in case I had an important meeting.

"I'm on my way," I told her. Mom has a way of not wanting to impose and so even emergencies are cloaked in the soft composure of her Midwestern tendency to not make a big scene when her husband snaps his tibia like a hard pretzel.

I walked into the bedroom of my parents house and found my Dad on the floor at the foot of the bed, clothed only in white briefs and a small plate of breakfast goodies, holding a glass of grape juice and reclining on his side like the lord of beige carpet. He had been woozy before falling and went to sit on the edge of the bed. He was eating to remedy the blood sugar level that perhaps caused his fall.   "Are you hurting?" I asked. "No, not really," said my Dad as he dangled the leg for me to see. I texted my brother, the physician from New York after we got to the hospital and sent him a picture of the leg with the caption, "His foot is floppin' like a mackerel on a hot deck."   "Isn't it too early to make light of the injury?", my brother texted back. I replied, "Yes...maybe, but the image just got into my head, sorry." Laughing through side-reclining pain on the carpet reminds me of a Soren Kierkegaard story about his dream of getting to heaven and having one wish to spend:

"A strange thing happened to me in my dream…I was granted the favor to have one wish…"Do you wish for youth, or for beauty, or power? Choose, but only one thing!" For a moment I was at a loss. Then I addressed the gods in this wise: "Most honorable contemporaries, I choose one thing — that I may always have the laughs on my side." Not one god made answer, but all began to laugh. From this I concluded that my wish had been granted and thought that the gods knew how to express themselves with good taste: for it would surely have been inappropriate to answer gravely: your wish has been granted." — Søren Kierkegaard

Many people have asked me, "How's your Dad doing?" I usually give the upbeat pc answer, but occasionally I tell the truth, "Terrible, he's not doing well," and the inquiring person looks surprised, like that wasn't what they expected to hear. Dad is 80, his bones are brittle, his heart is weak, and diabetes is relentless. And now he's working through physical therapy for six weeks doing exertions he couldn't do even before he broke the leg. So, yes, Dad is not doing well. But God still loves him, along with his family and friends, and he still has the wish of Kierkegaard, "…may I still have all the laughs on my side."

Dad is irreverent with his caregivers, but calls them by name and is considerate in his own ironic way, always looking for someone to laugh at his jokes, even though he's hurting. The nurse in charge of diet told him that he was 25 carb grams short of his daily goal and Dad told her that she could keep bringing it but that didn't mean he was going to eat it.

I remember what Dad did when he woke up from heart surgery fifteen years ago and found himself alive in the recovery room draped in devices and tubes…he sang, "Amazing Grace, how sweet the sound…", and when he left the hospital, we had instructions to go next door to the Olive Garden where we bought $200.00 worth of bread sticks and pasta and brought it back to the medical staff at St. John's. It was Dad's way of having the last laugh, of understanding that all the laughs were on his side.

Kierkegaard was not a cheery fellow. He said things like, "What if everything in the world were a misunderstanding, what if laughter were really tears?" Dad isn't Kierkegaard, he comes from the hills of Oklahoma near Bluejacket, where a yes is a yes and a handshake is a contract and pie suppers are "don't miss" social events…and where laughter rings out even in the darkest night.

Dad chooses to live as if laughter is reality, and the hospital nurse takes him in the wheelchair to the table for dinner as he sings Willie Nelson, "On the road again, I just can't wait to get on the road again."

Dad knows all the laughs are on his side.

41

How Deep the Father's Love for Us

"Hope is the thing with feathers
That perches in the soul
And sings the tune without the words
And never stops at all."
~ Emily Dickinson

Sunday morning during communion while the church sang, "How deep the Father's love for us," I sat and listened unable to sing, because I had a softball stuck in my throat. I had just read a text from my brother Toby, "Played a little chess Drew is beating me without even looking. Washing his hair this morning. The truck on top of the car dripped oil all over him...he is still hurting. On IV pain meds."

While the church sang...

"How great the pain of searing loss, The Father turns His face away, As wounds which mar the chosen One, Bring many sons to glory,"

...I thought about not being able to reach my own son, of Toby not being able to reach Drew, and of my own Father God, who could have reached his own Son, but used Divine restraint and only watched and saw the pain of searing loss.

I remember my brother lamenting the fact that he couldn't hold Drew when he was born because Drew was born prematurely. "I couldn't reach him, couldn't touch him, couldn't hold him." I'm not sure if my brother said those literal words, but that sense is what I've always remembered about the first few weeks of Drew's life. He was enclosed in glass for several weeks. Now he is a handsome young man, a chess player, a brilliant mathematician. Drew will be 22 on March 15th.

Last Friday night, he was in the back seat of a Subaru on I-71 near Louisville, and like his beginning in life, prone and asleep, enclosed in glass, but this time the glass and steel of a Subaru. His friend Nick drove and Nick's girlfriend, Abby Owens occupied the front passenger seat. A semi-truck and trailer skidding on snow and ice couldn't stop and plowed into the car, every parent's worst nightmare. We lost Nick, Abby was able to walk away, and for two hours, Drew was trapped in a tangle of steel, unable to move, legs pinned, with the oily sludge of an 18 wheeler dripping on him. Drew tried to move the weight that held him in a tight space, found it impossible, and calmed himself by praying and talking to Nick. He couldn't see Nick, but they talked, until Nick no longer was able to talk. Drew prayed. A paramedic came, and spoke with Drew. The paramedic prayed with Drew. And Drew waited in the freezing cold, covered in oil. Drew was at peace in God's hands.

And so Sunday morning, my brother the doctor, washed the oil from the hair of his son, as a thousand friends prayed, as total strangers offered the families places to stay, keys to cars for transportation around town, expressions of encouragement, food and money, hugs…and tears. They were covered with love from a great cloud of witnesses who believe in what these kids were doing. They were on their way to Syracuse to work with a church during spring break. Not the beach for spring break, not the mountains, they were going to be the hands and feet of Christ.

It was good to talk with Drew by phone last night and I told him if I was there, I'd kiss him on the head, and he said, "No thanks." And I knew he was going to be alright, because this world is not his home, he's just here for a while…like all of us really.

Thanks be to God that most of the time, we can reach our kids, touch them, love them, hold them, protect them. But when we can't, there are people out there behaving in ways that I can't entirely comprehend. God bless Nick, love him and hold him, Nick is home. I can't explain what happened at 1:15 AM March 7th on a cold interstate in Kentucky.

But I can explain what happened after, and it's the only thing that makes any sense.

42

Becky Ran Home Today

"How often do I stand in abject terror and raw trepidation before the impossible peaks that soar to impossible heights in front me, when God turns to me and calmly says "what mountains?"

~ Craig D. Lounsbrough

Becky Marie Davis ran home today. The last time she ran was 1954. But today, her legs were unbound, her lungs filled with fresh air, her heart soaked in heavens glory. As I watched the graceful withering of my Aunt Becky's physical nature I've observed the astounding levity of her soul. One can easily suggest that life treated her unfairly but she would be the last to say so. Coming home from the hospital this exchange occurred between her and the ambulance attendant. "Are you going home?" Never one to mince words, Becky answered: "I'm going home to wait on the Lord."

In an age of widespread entitlement, Becky never collected government disability and in a remarkable turn of grace, she was the source of charity rather than the recipient. I sat in Becky's living room visiting with her older sisters, Charlotte and Nordeen, just hours after her passing. Nordeen remarked, "Now I know why she paid so little income tax. She gave so much of her income away." Her life is even more remarkable when you know the rest of the story.

She was fifteen on Halloween day in 1954, the day Nordeen and Charlotte married Robert and Terrel in an authentic Depression-rooted-money-saving double wedding ceremony. Four weeks later she viewed visitors through an angled mirror as she lay on her back in an iron lung at Children's Hospital in Oklahoma City, telling jokes about the salesman startled by the woman opening the door. "You just about scared the pants off me lady!" To which the lady replied, "Boo, boo, boo!"

Humor wasn't the tenor of the times, however. American historian William O'Neill noted that, "Paralytic poliomyelitis was, if not the most serious, easily the most frightening public health problem of the post-war era." By 1952, polio was killing more children than any other communicable disease. Parents kept children home from school, avoided parks and swimming pools, and played only in small groups with the closest of friends.

At the age of fifteen, Becky was classically beautiful, spry, and energetic with curly black hair and dark sparkling eyes and a slim figure. The Halloween wedding was a platform for flirtation with boys while she served punch. Her body, her beauty, her face, her soul, were all shaped by polio, and the beauty that defined her at fifteen starkly contrasted the beauty that defined here at sixteen and beyond. And yet, her beauty grew deeper, more elegant, more soulful with each advancing year. Fifty-nine years hence, Charlotte and Nordeen sat in her living room contemplating the wonder of her remarkable temperament, her refusal to accept pity, her abundant generosity, her choice to live beyond the crutch of complaint with class and dignity.

She would return from the hospital to her home northeast of Boise City, OK in the summer of 1955, carried from the car to the house by her brother-in-law, Terrel, braces framing her withered legs, the effects of polio dictating a tyranny of physical limitations for the rest of her life. I saw what she looked like in 1955 even though I was not yet born. The vision I saw was one of the most famous paintings by a U.S. artist in the 20th century.

Andrew Wyeth painted a picture called *Christina's World*. Christina Olson was Wyeth's neighbor in Maine and he painted the picture in 1948 using Christina as a model. Christina was a polio victim and unable to walk, spending much of her time near her home at Cushing, Maine. The resemblance to Becky is stunning. It could have been my aunt Becky lying in a dry field in the Panhandle of Oklahoma, facing her house, longing to run home on sturdy legs.

Becky endured eight months at Children's Hospital and then at a convalescence home rehabilitating. Becky spent the next year learning to walk and breath and live again. She never wanted pity, never complained, always feared herself a burden. Her life has been a picture of determination, grace, hard work, grit, strength and love.

I look at Wyeth's picture of Christina and see Becky in 1955. Her atrophied legs splayed behind her unable to walk…her life before her but still unsure how to run home. Her black hair, the bend of her elbow, the distinctive paralytic distortion of the spine. Unlike Christina, Aunt Becky would walk again, after a time of healing and rehabilitation. It's a wonder she survived the 325 mile ambulance ride from Boise City to Oklahoma City via two lane highways at 100 m.p.h. speeds, with her parents, Jess and Mildred, frantically trying to keep pace, unsure of the fate of their daughter. A common image of the early 1950's was of a father carrying a limply draped daughter or son, limbs flaccid and flopping as he walked grimly, helplessly, wondering if their child would live or die.

I never saw Becky run. I never saw convulsing fall-down-on-the-ground laughter (she laughed with a kind of expelled air wheezing that marked the limits of her lung capacity). I never saw her walk without her halting lyrically determined high-kneed gait. I have tried to see Becky as she looked during the summer of 1954 rather than the summer of 1955. Climbing trees, falling off corral fences breaking her arm, always curious, never limited by gravity or oxygen or withered legs. But that wouldn't be true to her nature, that wouldn't be true to the story she wrote with the rest of her life. The rest of her story began in 1955. She was unlucky. She was the only child anyone could remember in the Boise City area to contract polio during that time and the Salk vaccine was approved for safe use just months after she contracted the virus with widespread immunization beginning in April 1955. Salk actually vaccinated his family and a few researchers in 1952, and over one million children in 1954, but the fully approved injectable dead-virus form of immunization wouldn't be administered to the broad population of the U.S. until April 1955. Just a few months later and Becky would have been immunized from this terrifying viral infection.

Becky Davis

It's difficult for those born post-1955 to understand the terror of that time, especially for parents of children at risk. I recently read a letter written by Becky's mom, my Grandma Mildred. She wrote, "...I guess I never stopped to question those things happening...thinking of some of the times I have been most afraid, I think of Becky having polio." Grandma, like Aunt Becky, was never one for melodrama. She simply let her yes be yes and her no was no. Her terror? "I think of Becky having polio..." Grandma lived through the environmental and economic disaster of the Dust Bowl, two world wars, and FDR's comforting national encouragement, "the only thing to fear is fear itself". Yet, Grandma's biggest fear was losing Becky.

Becky's adventurous spirit belied the meek and gentle bent of her personality. She once broke an arm climbing on the back of her high chair as a toddler. Later, walking the top of the corral fence in a contest to see who could keep their balance without falling, she fell. As Charlotte hurried her to the house for treatment of another broken arm, Becky told Charlotte to calm down and slow down. She's been doing that ever since, a calming influence, slowing us down, putting us in our place, knocking us off our high horse. Becky's wounds and the challenges she endured didn't define her, but they did frame her indomitable personality. To imagine her physically perfect is an exercise in futility because that wasn't her. She was a *wounded healer*....like Jesus. The pain she endured, rehabilitation, learning to walk and breath, the power of her quiet strength through suffering, were part of what made her so wonderful.

Not to mention she drove the coolest cars, cars her nieces and nephews coveted, cars which became her running legs. It was her way of overcoming Newton's 1st Law of Physics, the tendency of a body at rest to remain at rest unless acted on by an outside force. She broke the law binding her legs using a Pontiac 455 HO engine under the hood of her 1970 gold GTO. It was her windows down, wind in my hair, get-outta-my-way, I'm finishing the walk around the corral fence moment.

A few days before she died, my brother Greg said to her, "God is pleased with you." Becky responded, "How do you know?" *How do we know?* We don't presume to be the judge and jury, but this we know. Becky managed her financial life with self-sufficiency and generosity. She lived within her means and was never a burden to anyone financially. She was the source of more than her share of household income and was a constant companion to my Grandma Mildred and later to sister Jessie. She gave money to those in need and an inordinately large amount of her earnings to the Dewey Church, missionaries and orphanages. She taught 3rd grade Bible school class. She worked with World Bible School ministry for many years. But she never had any sense that she was contributing anything more than what she was supposed to be contributing. She always deflected, always pushed aside praise.

Just days before she passed I sat with her and asked her about teaching 3rd graders. She said, "I need you to gather all the third graders together." I asked, "Why?" She replied, "I need to apologize for my bad teaching. I really struggled to explain things to third graders." Then she told me this story. She was teaching about local church autonomy and asked a young boy where the headquarters of the Church was located. He replied, "In Elder Charlie Tucker's office."

She understood her teaching, her giving, her service, her work, her family, were all gifts of grace, just as her life was a gift and even though she suffered, through it all she taught us about grace, about how the wounded have the greatest capacity to heal.

My brother Greg was in Becky's hospital room with Ralph Jackson, one of the elders from Becky's church. Ralph said, "Becky is a classy lady. She has a queenly nature about her." Ralph's right, but I'm guessing that queenly crown is going to have to wait a bit. Becky is climbing every tree in sight, chasing every rabbit, running home through the field, her dark hair flowing behind her like windswept wheat. Becky ran home today and I don't think she'll stop for a long time.

43

The Heavens and Dark Matter

Miracles are a retelling in small letters of the very same story which is written across the whole world in letters too large for some of us to see.

~ C.S. Lewis

In the black curtained film room of Limestone Grade School, I traveled through space riding a projector beam, like Slim Pickens in Dr. Strangelove astride a flying nuclear warhead, as educational brilliance shone through dancing classroom lint. We sat with eyes pinned to the screen, our tickets punched as we left our protestant white middle class sameness and ventured out into the world. The chattering projector sang with the benevolent narrator who knew everything from the orbital position of protons to the gross national product of Mozambique. The narrator was a mentor, a voice in my world of certitude and scientific reason. Reasons assured voice spoke through the chatter of the projector and set itself on my shoulder like a gargoyle on a cathedral, an ancient muse speaking truth in the measured voice of a middle-aged white man in thick black glasses wearing a tweed suit and skinny tie.

That voice of the intellectual arch angel sitting on one shoulder was not unopposed. The angel of rebellion sitting on my other shoulder kept me guessing. Like the Fiddler on the Roof, trying to scratch out a simple tune while keeping my balance astride a steep roof, I listened to advocates and raconteurs, the voices of measured reason and the voices of unbridled trouble, an angel and a punk, shouting shoulder to shoulder across the breadth of my face. They shouted through my ears on Earth day and when we toured the Zinc smelters and the room of mainframe computers at Phillips 66 corporate headquarters. Hushed whispers and shouting argued for the romance of technology and progress against a good earth preacher condemning jaded capitalism and environmental nihilism.

The skeptical party angel was Alfred E. Neuman, the cover boy of Mad Magazine, with jug ears, a missing front tooth and one eye slightly lower than the other, mischief written on his magnificent forehead. The narrator from the educational films was the good guy, the one with all the correct answers, an announcer to my orthodox world formed inside the womb of social, educational, and religious traditions.

The battle between orthodoxy and mischief, altruism and gratification, reason and unhinged emotion, still echoes today, although the battle lines are askew and not always defined as elegantly as by the film narrator and Alfred E. Neuman. But the arguments still roar unabated across the vast plain of consciousness that is my mind, my community, my world. I relate to the Apostle Paul, in his perplexing self-assessment of why he's sometimes soft-headed and at other times stubborn, "I do not do what I want to do, and I do the things I hate."

I've observed this dichotomy while watching moonwalks and presidential assassinations, experiencing seasons of faith and doubt. Now, I feel closer to the moon and stars than to the trajectory of an assassin's bullet, more nigh to faith than doubt. But the light and dark still fight for space in my mind. And in the midst of the fight, even in dark moments, like watching the shining film in my grade school screening room, I think of heaven.

My whimsical childhood view of heaven was Disneyland (exorcised of, *It's a Small World After All,* which undoubtedly plays a relentless loop in hell). Shortly thereafter, I began to ask questions. Is Heaven trash free, cobbled streets of gold, minions and rubes always smiling, people of no particular distinction, all ethnicities boarding rides, a never-ending Space Mountain roller coaster, every dip a thrill, each turn surreal?

Once I ruled out Disneyland, within moments of doubt, The Who's line, *"I hope I die before I get old"*, seemed plausible. Don't get me wrong, I always wanted to die at an old age and go to Heaven, but my passion for Heaven was not equal to the lady in the feathered box hat blocking my view of a preacher imploring me to get right and ready to go home. I didn't understand Heaven in the theological sense, and I felt no longing for streets of gold, preferring dirt and asphalt, highway stripes streaming under my spinning wheels.

However, the older I get, the more I feel Heaven in my bones and it feels like Bing Crosby singing White Christmas, something magical, the warmth of a fireplace and stockings hung, family together, relationships whole, twinkling beauty alongside a peace that passes understanding. A yearning for something ancient and familiar, even though I've no idea what it is, I peer through a glass obscured by the profane, seeing the magical holy in rare moments collected in pans of swirling water and dirt, a miner panning for gold.

I felt these moments as a youngster, although I had no language to describe them. This yearning was shaped like a highway ribbon, sounded like a train in a river gorge, and felt like a hiking trail underfoot leading to a peaceful ledge in the clouds. Those pathways to somewhere vibrated with the music of freedom. Freedom from what I had no idea, but with rolled down windows and hair flapping in the wind like an anthem, I longed for independence. Heaven seemed to be waiting down by the tracks where the streets were darker, yet exhilarating, unlike the Disneyesque streets of conformed wonder.

As a young CPA working in Collingswood, New Jersey in 1987, on a lunch excursion with my Jersey buddies, we experienced one of these ethereal moments sitting in a car rather than church pews. We were rolling down the White Horse Pike on our way to the King of Pizza when Bruce Springsteen's *Thunder Road* leaped from our radio like the Star Spangled Banner, and we saluted and sang ourselves into exultation, four guys singing off key at full macho volume, "roll down the window and let the wind blow back your hair..." I was initiated into the fraternity of The Boss, and for two minutes, that seemed like heaven. Perfect and emotionally connected, on the same page, tuned in, crazy, wondrous. It was a moment of connection, a fully alive moment, one of simultaneous peace and exhilaration. We were one in the moment, young and erudite, exultantly together, bullet-proof against the world of whatever may come.

I love those moments, the invasion of hope pushing aside despair, goodness washing away malice. The subtle announcement is here and there, a fascination with the sky, the first heaven, a place filled with sonic booms, baseballs leaving yards, geese flying south, and like the dark matter confounding today's scientists, something in the air, something not yet imagined. I was a dogboy in a truck window, tongue out and eyes shut against the highway breeze, with no idea of the destination.

I sensed this atmosphere as a canvas, a seedbed to cultivate wonder out of which grew masterpieces of childhood imagination, including war games along wooded creeks and sidewalks chalked with business plans to cover the neighborhood with lemonade stands. We painted our canvas with pigment flowing from vats of boredom.

It was my first heaven, a place filling our lungs with oxygen and our eyes with a sky of Air Force blue brushed with ribbons of jet contrail, a space we filled with Superman, pollution, and everlasting optimism. In that atmosphere we were untethered, floating in our own space/time of creation enabled by a world that was bigger in the sense that we were further apart, blissfully unaware that the world wide web was being created by the binary engineering of Moore's law. In our ignorance of space and time we were allowed to cure our own boredom.

We watched Walter Cronkite interrupt *As the World Turns*, "President Kennedy died at one p.m. central standard time," then take off his thick black glasses and pause for five seconds to gather his emotion, put the glasses back on and try to speak again, emotion choking the words he said next, "Vice-President Johnson…". We all knew right where we were at that moment, because it felt easier to be one and our grief and sorrow was united along with our sense of injustice and helplessness.

We watched the nightly news, Jennings on ABC, Cronkite on CBS, Huntley and Brinkley on NBC, as they delivered news in images and sound bites, three town criers behind the network curtain. I saw revolutionaries yelling at America to pay no attention to those men behind the curtain. The hum of change drifted in the air like high voltage wires pulsing between our ears trying to obscure the sounds of tradition which we still heard comfortably. Those sounds of tradition were what connected us, our version of a smaller wireless world.

Our neighborhood volume elevated on Saturday. We weren't immersed in unique playlists with headphones, we shared each other's noise like the constant droning of lawn mowers and Bob Barry's staccato radio call of an Oklahoma touchdown coming from Mr. Johnson's garage and the lyrical droning of cicadas as they turned their vibrating tymbals to lazy summer volume.

I collected those sounds in my memory like my friends collected 45 rpm records, a touch of Nascar, a bit of Animal Planet, a stirring of ABC's Wide World of Sports giving inspiration to our drama of athletic competition written into backyards while Howard Cosell called our play-by-play.

From the Warner's garage came the plea of summer in the amplified guitar riffs of the local band dreaming of screaming teenage girls and the Ed Sullivan show. A Shelby Mustang sounded of rich testosterone on a Friday night at the Sonic drive-in, a Yamaha 65 motorcycle with a duct-taped seat the sound of the unwashed incessant, unwilling to cede the neighborhood throne of macho to the privileged few. There is the hiss of the mosquito truck spewing a final solution white fog into our worldly aspirations as mosquitos go limp like marathoners hitting the finish line. The wind rustles crimson and orange notes, winters gentle hint in the hills of oak and maple framing ramps of asphalt.

The creeks teem with crawdads chased by tireless young hands, Godzilla chasing victims onto the beach stirring muddy bottoms and minnows into distressed eddies of malted milk. Bermuda lawns are dotted with limestone outcroppings where grass refuses to grow and no kid dares to go barefoot, as goat heads propagate like rabbits while kids guard their feet with P.F. flyers and Chuck Taylor high-tops. I smelled people living all around me, burning leaves, freshly cut grass, lawn mower fumes and charcoal burning in backyards.

Roaming a nearby dump with my neighbor Dale, we discovered a baby blue plastic chair, body-conforming, chrome-legged right off the set of the Brady Bunch, which we claimed and toted home. Watching with amazement, Dale took a rock and hammered a hole in the seat, then threaded a stick and rope through to the bottom of the chair then flung the other rope end up and over the meaty limb of a massive oak that reigned majestically on the edge of our yard. After cinching the chair to the proper height and tying it off, he said, "Hop on," as I stood looking at this great Modern plastic wonder. This was not my grandfather's tire swing. It was designed by Andy Warhol and built without a blueprint using the tools of time and boredom.

I asked in a tone of awe, "How did you do that?", "Good 'ole American ingenuity," came the reply. I told Dale, "I'm American and a genius, but I couldn't make that!" He just laughed and we began swinging ourselves high into the Oklahoma sky under this great oak. We soon turned up the adrenaline by using a Schwinn Fair Lady bike with the wicker handlebar basket removed, Dale pedaling furiously down the hill as I grabbed the rope from my perch on the front handlebars while sliding into the seat in one motion, defying common sense but trusting in the physics of youthful eye and hand timing, sprinkled with a touch of angel dust, our top speed providing the force to fling us past parallel as the bike continued on down the hill, and I peered straight down into the lawn at great height until feeling a slack in the rope, then retracing the arc of the swing in a tic toc that gradually lowered my racing heart.

We also knew how to slow down before New Age mysticism made it fashionable and high blood pressure prescribed it. In our void of activity, like the rope swing at its zenith we sought our inevitable nadir of tension, we went slack and quieted our young minds like the gradual slowing of the swing, just letting gravity and a little lemonade and shade slow us down as we quit chasing and let life come to us. We relaxed in the cool canopy of a forked elm tree which we called the *Shady Rest*, and from that shady hangout, I saw places and moments.

Just down the street from the elm tree is an oily spot in the asphalt where Charlie Harris poured gasoline and then tossed a match just to watch energy burn in the street, and where we rode our bikes around a 1922 silver dollar imbedded in the neighbor's driveway using it as a lap marker. The Harris family never locked their front door allowing Jana Wilkins to sleepwalk into their parlor late one night. Further east is a gravel road through the woods leading to a hangout where kids smoked cigarettes at the perpetual campfire flickering from an old gas wellhead. This was the atmosphere that we lived in, our neighborhood.

According to an ancient way of explaining the atmosphere, humans occupy the first heaven. We don't live beneath the sky, we live in it. It was in this first heaven that I bought Jolly Ranchers and Atomic Fire Balls at the Ben Franklin 5 & 10. And it was in this first heaven that I saw people hurt badly for the first time, a car wreck down the street exploded our quiet world and we sprinted to see the girl sitting in the ditch while someone placed a blanket over her shaking shoulders.

Once I peered through the first heaven and into the second, looking for the man on the moon. Sunday evening, July 20, 1968, I stepped out of the back seat of a white 1968 Buick Electra and saw Neil Armstrong, who once told unfunny jokes about the moon following them with the real punch line, "Aaahh...I guess you had to be there." Our driveway was surrounded by a cluster of scrub oak so I walked out to the center of our yard to escape the trees, and I peered into the evening sky as it collected an orange creamsicle/blue-sky day and mingled it with shades of gray and black melding into dusty shades of infinite space. I saw Neil Armstrong in the Sea of Tranquility planting the American flag in moon cheese. At least I thought it was him. The shadows may have fooled me.

I rushed inside to confirm my suspicions and watched a black and white TV image of Eric Sevareid declare, "We've seen some kind of birth here." Sevareid, the CBS commentator, described Armstrong's clumsy first moments on strange ground as a "clumsy creature, half-blind, maneuvering with great awkwardness at first, and slowly learning to use its legs, until, in a rather short time it's running."

Mr. Sevareid could just as easily been describing me, growing up in the schoolyard down the street where I was taught to climb under the desk and curl into a tight ball on my knees and cover my head in the event of a nuclear blast, clumsy, half-blind, maneuvering with great awkwardness at first, then emerging from beneath my desk to peer into the atmosphere, through the mushroom cloud of humanity to find heaven, a place where I could drive on gilded streets in golf carts like Mickey in the Magic Kingdom.

The ancients thought of the heavens in three senses. Neil Armstrong has seen the first two heavens, our atmosphere and the space beyond the air we breathe, but he hasn't seen the third. I haven't seen the third Heaven, but I have seen the flashes of brilliance, the intersections of the holy with the profane, heaven's dimensional plane overlapping the grimy yet whimsically beautiful world of earth and sea, fire and sky.

The third heaven is both here and now, there and then. A present reality, and unveiled mystery. Now it's clearly seen in the birth of my children and the gentle hope-filled death of my loved ones, and then it's veiled in the mystery of the greedy and hopeless, the addicted and starving. One day the veil will reveal what can't be seen clearly and completely. Perhaps the third heaven is the dark matter I couldn't see, but felt, as a kid growing up in the first heaven of a neighborhood in the middle of America.

The third heaven is a place I've imagined but have seen only in flashes of brilliance in the first heaven. The third heaven feels like a place where swings never go slack and our walks are wide-eyed, a place where canopied trees are shared and the perpetual flame of restoration burns. A place where garage bands sound better than the Beatles and where Ed Sullivan stands and applauds for a really good show. I dream often of the third heaven.

I'm a dreamer. Not so much in the romantic mode of Don Quixote, but rather, in the way all humans experience dreams. But I rarely remember them. So, when a dream enters my dream bibliography and I capture it before it escapes into the steam of my morning coffee, it leaves a mark. I'm haunted by one, and restored by another.

One night, not far from celebrating our thirtieth wedding anniversary, I dreamed that I died. And like Lazarus, I arose. It was on the patio of our home that I saw her. My wife looked different, but it was her, and elated, I quickly walked to Karen with outstretched arms. She was walking to me and I knew her, but her eyes were unblinking crystals, and she walked through me like a deer walking through morning fog. She didn't know me, and we were separated by an unnamed invisible wall. I instantly felt sad, alone, separated from the woman I've shared life with for thirty years. And then I woke up, for real this time, and she was there in bed, beside me, and I was relieved and happy. To be totally alone, without touch, without the soft voice of conversation and love, to be invisible, stunned me, made me hurt, made me lonely.

The second dream is a conglomeration of dreams and it begins in a sea of failure, and ends in revelation. In this dream, I'm writing a book. I've spent my whole life trying to write, to create sentences that resonate, that leap off bright pages and into dark souls. I have high expectations, but disappointment and discouragement are the product of my work. So much unfinished, so much to be done. I'm distracted from writing my book, distracted by my children as I read to them and go to their games, burdened by shopping lists that require me to search for kale and escarole, detoured by employees who require a pay check every Friday. I'm so undone by it all. I never can finish my work. Like in the other dream, I die and go to another world. Standing before the elders, I hold in my hand the product of my life, one page. The best I could do was one page. I look up from the one page I hold in my hand and notice that we are in a library. The library is never ending and it is the most beautiful place I've ever seen and the books are tenderly worn, the loving patina of those who read with understanding. No bindings are broken, no books are tattered, no words are faded. And I'm standing in a section with all the books I've ever dreamed of reading and writing.

And I realize that one page was enough. The people around me were dreamers also, the plumbers, teachers, coaches, lawyers, artists, athletes, all were dreamers. They were also writing their page, their own vision. Justice and beauty and relationship, all written down on these pages in a perfect library and it is complete, filled with knowledge, the lion reading with the lamb, the broken now healed in a library of perfect bindings and marvellous pages telling the story of a kingdom of brave deeds.

And I realize, finally, that I am home.

Made in the USA
Lexington, KY
18 May 2017